A Walk
Up The Green

by
Gary Smith

Winson Green House situated across the road from the prison. (Photograph - Kensington Museum)

A Walk
Up The Green

by

Gary Smith

with
Foreword by

Dr. Carl Chinn

BREWIN BOOKS

First published April 1999
by Brewin Books, Doric House, Church Street,
Studley, Warwickshire.

ISBN 1 85858 142 7

British Library Cataloguing-in-Publication Data.
A catalogue record for this book is available from the British Library.

Typeset in Clearface and
made and printed in Great Britain
by SupaPrint (Redditch) Limited,
Redditch, Worcestershire

FOREWORD

Carl Chinn

Each of us has made history. Each of us has a tale to tell. Each of us have feelings to pour forth. Yet too few of us recognise the importance of the stories of our lives – and if we do, too many of us have too little time or too little opportunity to pass on to the next generation what we have done and how we have felt. Gary Smith is a person who has recognised not only the significance of the events with which he has been involved but also has decided to pass them on. His first book, *Winson Green – My World*, brought to the fore his experiences. More than that, his work highlighted the need to view The Green as one of Brum's major working-class heartlands. So successful was he in reaching out to others the many Winson Greenites have been inspired to write to Gary about themselves. The result is this new book, *A Walk Up The Green*, in which the folk of the Green write about their families, their streets and their neighbourhood. The world so many of us grew up in becomes more distant each year. As the new millennium approaches it is vital we do not let ourselves and our people disappear beneath the ocean of history. Gary Smith has made his contribution to this task. Why can't you?

CONTENTS

INTRODUCTION

When I started my first book "Winson Green My World" I didn't think that I would ever start another. The area I wrote about was only a small part of Winson Green. Naturally, I knew the Green well and the shops and streets that went off Winson Green Road too, but not the people, and where and how they lived. As I have said previously, I was lucky that the back-house I was brought up in had a front garden and a back yard. Up the Green they weren't so lucky. The area from Dudley Road down towards Smethwick was soon to be filled with a ribbon of streets and houses.

Being encompassed by a main road on one side and a canal and railway on the other meant squashing in as much property as possible in the middle, which consequentially meant a lot of over crowded dwellings. Even though at the bottom of the Green in Wellington Street and also Foundry Road there were back-to-back houses, they weren't so predominant as in some of the streets up the Green. I make this point for it will become evident as this story unfolds. While I was writing my first book "Winson Green My World" people I had never met made contact with me telling me stories of their lives up the Green and some of the areas of my district. It was the basis of these stories which decided me to at least attempt this book. I am grateful to the host of people who gave me information, photos and of course answers to my many questions. I thank them all most sincerely for the help they gave me. These people didn't know me, but they wanted someone to put their stories and reminiscences down on paper and to tell others about where they lived, the characters, the shops, the pubs and of course about the ups and downs in their lives.

This book is the second part of a trilogy, there is one area still to do, that is Lodge Road, only when I have written that third book will my story of Winson Green be complete.

So, this second part of my story unfolds about an area which was originally part of the area called the "Heath" and which later became Heath Street, with all around it growing upwards and outwards.

ACKNOWLEDGEMENTS

This book would probably never have been started without people such as Pat Smith (no relation), she herself was born in Heath St, her name then was Dimmock. She had been in touch with me at the time of writing my first book, her memories and tales started me off. Also to Jim Wilson, his help with the knowledge on the area was incredible and coming out Heath St as well really got me going. Also thanks to Dave Avery, Hilda Thomas, Alan Dolman, Johnnie Landon who provided some marvellous photo's and as usual my dear friend Paula who corrects my English. There are many others though who contributed to this book. To them all I want to say a big thank you. Also the one who had to suffer once again, whom I might add, is the power behind the pen, my wife Margaret. There is one other person whom I would like to thank and that is our own Carl Chinn, thanks mate.

DEDICATION

To my mom. A typical Brummie, short on words, quick on action. She was born in Aberdeen St, christened at St Cuthberts. If it hadn't been for the Great War, and our gran taking her and our uncle Bill to live with her parents in Wellington St. I would have gone to Dudley and Barford Road Schools. I would have played around the 'feeder', and made my hunting ground around the Dudley Road area. This wasn't to be. But I can now put the record straight. This is for her and the rest that came from up the Green.

Chapter 1
From Summer Hill Road to Winson Green

Between 1825 and 1850, Birmingham spread westward from Great Hampton Row past what is now Hockley. In the early 1700's Matthew Boulton had moved from his small factory in Snow Hill to possibly the largest factory, at that time, in the western hemisphere. It was situated at Gib Heath, an area between Winson Green and Handsworth. Not to be outdone, the sons of Boulton and Watt decided that the factory at Soho, Handsworth needed more space and better provision for moving their goods. The great canal navigator Brindley provided the means of easier transportation of their goods. He had built the Birmingham and Wolverhampton canal in 1769. What could be better, and cheaper than paying duties on toll roads, than a canal barge moving vast amounts of goods by water. Others in turn decided to follow suit, land was cheap, all it needed was a work-force, but we will go on with that a bit later.

Birmingham to the west had two major roads, Soho Road (which was formerly known as Wednesbury Road), and Dudley Road. Both of these roads were tolled, but the canal, and later the railway, made these tolls obsolete. The Soho foundry in Smethwick filled in the space between Icknield Street and Staffordshire. Along the route of the canal towpath other factories were to rise. All these factories needed workers, and more importantly, somewhere for them to live. Streets and roads would have to be built, and because of the need for many workers, many many houses would have to be compressed into a small area.

Winson Green was no different from any other city or large town. It had the same hard working people living in the back-to-back housing squalor and the same impoverished living conditions. What we didn't realise, however, is that we were at the heart of the industrialised world. Birmingham the city of a thousand trades. Not that it would have seemed of importance to somebody bringing up eight children.

The Winson Green area gained prominence with the building of the prison, the workhouse and the mental asylum in the 1850's. Winson Green was something of a misnomer, the centre of which, we must never forget, was the prison and the workhouse, if not in actual geographical terms then certainly in the minds of the people. The prison was built on the through road between Handsworth and Edgbaston, and if it had not been for the notoriety of those two institutions, the area would just have been an hodge podge of factories, shops and people. At least these dreaded institutions were always a good talking point for our area.

Metal bashing and other heavy industry would push up from Smethwick. With Nettlefolds becoming the front runner. After which other factories would spring up, as we shall see as our story unfolds.

Another main thoroughfare was Dudley Road which was the continuation of Spring Hill and went on to Oldbury in Staffordshire. Up until the late 1700's, the area just off Dudley Road and Spring Hill, known as Brookfields, was no more than an extension of the Heath. Land, as I have previously written about in my first book, was owned either by Sir Thomas Gooch, Colonel Vyse and the Debirmingham family and other wealthy land owners. It would have consisted of smallholdings, and a smattering of cottage industries with houses dotted around. It was just off the Heath and was also arable land, but all that was to change. To a traveller, at the end of the 1840's, making his way up Spring Hill from the town, the fields as such were disappearing as the ribbon of streets, shops and houses began reaching out from Icknield Street. As he climbed the hill he would have passed the old college which, in later years, would be a public house bearing the same name. If he had looked over the bridge at the top of Spring Hill he would have seen the canal, this part being a loop from the main canal from Smethwick. This branch of the canal twisted and turned from just above the new Borough Goal, and made its way through the grounds of the asylum, a joint then went off towards Soho Pool. After that the line carried on towards All Saints, up through Brookfields passing the said college, back under Dudley Road, at the side of what was later to become Barker and Allen's factory, and then on to Edgbaston Reservoir. The reservoir was built not only as a storage of fresh water but also kept the canal filled up to its proper level. The canal then went back to the main line opposite Stour Street. Barker and Allen's factory came later, at this time it was a glass works. The land was sold by a J. Woodcock to a glass maker in 1786. Work in the glass making trade was prevalent in the Birmingham area, probably due to the amount of sand Birmingham was built on! In 1904, after the glass works ceased to operate, the land was sold again, this time it was to be known as the German Silver Works. After this Barker and Allen's came into the picture. Anyway, to get back to the story, our traveller would see the building of the new workhouse, impressive in its size as it stretched from Dudley Road to the bottom of Western Road. Was this huge workhouse a sign of the times and a possible omen for the future? From looking over the canal bridge our traveller would carry on along Dudley Road, branching off the the right was Heath Street, this is where our story really starts.

In the 1840's one would see building taking place all along Dudley Road, the fields being taken over by man's need for more and more housing. Factories in the distance would be pouring out smoke from their tall chimney stacks. Heath Street would be no more than a narrow lane which ran down from the Dudley Road to the boundary of Smethwick. This though would change dramatically as we shall see. On his walk along the Dudley Road, the next street our traveller would come to was the Winson Green Road, which in turn crossed Heath Street. He was in no doubt that the new Borough Gaol was being built at the bottom of this road, as with a shiver he crossed the road. On he would go past what was going to become Dudley Road Board School and down the Dudley Road to Smethwick. On the left hand side were green fields leading across to Edgbaston. On this side of the road were still pockets of open land but slowly and surely they were to be built on, and he would have had no idea in the space of about 20 years thousands of people and hundreds of dwelling houses would be squeezed into this small area.

Looking up the "Green" in the 60's.
The Smith's Arms on the left.
(A. Dolman)

3

Chapter 2
From out of Heath Street to the top of the Green

Possibly no other town had the fortune, or perhaps the misfortune, to have a prison, a hospital, a mental asylum, a fever hospital and the dreaded workhouse all in one area and virtually on the same site. It all started with the prison being built in 1849. The old Borough Gaol (which we shall go into later in the book) in the centre of town had outgrown it's usefulness, and as more space was needed for the erection of a much bigger and more secure establishment, what could be better than part of the Heath, well it was no use for anything else. A couple of years later came the "Lunatic Asylum", a dreadful title which, thankfully over the years, has gradually changed to "Mental Hospital". The workhouse came next closely followed by the fever hospital in 1853. It wasn't till 1869 that the workhouse expanded and an infirmary was added. This huge municipal undertaking needed even more people to service it, as did the factories which were springing up all around. Streets were built with grand and proud names, Aberdeen, Carlisle, Peel and Lansdowne, all famous politicians. Field Marshalls Wellington and Kitchener were also honoured in this way. Sadly though, there weren't tree lined avenues but rows upon rows of terraced and back-to-back houses. Only one street took it's name from the area that was Heath Street, which was a short cut to Smethwick, and which saved the need to travel the full length of Dudley Road to get there. Heath Street came off Dudley Road at an angle and made it's way down towards Smethwick and Boulton and Watt's new factory at Soho. Later there were to be other huge factories such as Tangyes and the biggest of them all Nettlefold and Chamberlain. Later to be known as the G.K.N. Many of the workers for these came from the Black Country with their skills of ironwork. Artisans and labourers alike made their way from far and near in need of work and the hope of a better life. Streets sprang up all around, Tudor (originally called Green Street), Cuthbert, Molliet and Abberley streets, all built for the want of land. It was an open house as free-holders sold their ground and builders to make as much for a quick profits and gains. Even in the 1850's the word "jerry builder" was used! The people were only too happy to be earning regular wages, even if they were crammed together like cattle in farmyards. They forgave all this and made the best they could of their lives, they like the thousands of other across Britain were prepared to accept this so that their children might reap the

4

benefit of their struggles. Unfortunately it would take more than one generation to climb up that ladder.

So our story of a walk "up the Green" continues as we go down Heath Street. I know we have gone passed Aberdeen street but that street is included in our tour later. On the corner of Heath Street and Dudley Road we have the Lea Bridge Tavern. Where was the "lea" in this area? The bridge yes, that made sense as the bridge over the railway and the Grand Union Canal stood right by, but the "lea" was probably an early gimmick by the brewers who owned the tavern to make the people think they were in the countryside. There were some lovely houses on the right hand side going down Heath Street. White brickwork following the ground and first floor windows, and at each of the sills of the bedroom and attic windows attractive patterned brickwork. This type of house went all the way down the right hand side as far as Winson Green Road. Going back to the top though on the right hand side on the corner of Dudley Road was a record shop. As a young man it was the only place locally to buy the latest records. It was worth the walk up the Green to this shop. Climax Radio, a name that will always stick out in my memory, as it will for many of us from that area.

The houses on the left hand side were less attractive and didn't have the fancy decoration or brickwork. Not every builder had the foresight to make buildings noticeable. About a third of the way down Heath Street we have the crossroads with Winson Green Road. Turn to the right and on that corner was Ward's High Class Grocers. They even sold wine loose from the barrel. When I was little I would go "up the Green" with my dad or one of my aunts to buy a couple of bottles of "loose" Tarrogona wine for Christmas. I eventually found out that it was some sort of port. If I remember rightly the hand painted sign advertising Tarragona wine was still on the side of the wall when the buildings were knocked down many years later. Next door to Ward's came Wm. Beck and Sons the chemists who dispensed all the locals' medicines and remedies. That was the last of the buildings until we head past the canal bridge and Winson Green Railway Station and going on further would bring you to the prison at the bottom. Turn to the left from Heath Street into Winson Green Road and you would be heading up to Summerfield Park, not a bad difference! On the other corner of Heath Street was the Shakespeare public house. Then as we go up Winson Green Road all manner of shops are to be found, everything from a dressmaker to a corn and seed merchant. Who, I wonder, remembers Ferranti Ltd the radio repair shop (was this the real Ferranti?), next door to this was Mrs. Lawrence, a much favoured fish and chip shop, a couple of sweet shops, Robotham's and Mrs. Williams. There was a china shop kept by Herbert Deakin, Lucy Best the draper had two shops one at number 9 and the other at 43. The men's barber was Mills's and the ladies hairdresser was Mr. Frederick Upcott (probably an early Mr. Teazy Weazy). All these shops, and a few more besides were between numbers 3 to 51. Evans's who kept the flower shop, Mrs.

5

May Hobden who had 'the dining rooms', and your newspapers would have come from Walter Browning's the newsagent. If a "smoke" was to your taste then all your requisites were available from Henry Turner at number 45. There were so many shops at the top of "the Green", this was as far as you would need to go for almost any of your requirements. Half a pound of sprouts it was Crathorne's, and a bag of sugar?, then Farmer's or Edith and Alice Payne's was the place. The variety of shops was vast, even the many pigeon fanciers were catered for at Ernie Painting's corn and seed shop. He was a relation of the man who became a front runner to the Merry Hill Social in Wellington Street. If their watches stopped whilst waiting for the pigeons to come home, then Frederick Mee the watch and clock repairer was just next door to come to their assistance. I could go on, from Deakin the china dealer and Bill Jones the cycle shop owner, this pattern was to be continued both ways along Dudley Road, towards Spring Hill to the left and to Smethwick to the right.

On the corner of Northbrook Street, the terminus of the 95 bus route, there was a little shop owned and run by the Misses Rice, three spinsters who were compassionate in one way but also very businesslike. They, like many other small shops in Birmingham, would sell clothes "on tick" and many of the hard-up people of the area would have used their shop, and probably would have pretended they had bought the clothes from a shop in the town. Another important shop on Dudley Road, opposite Icknield Port Road, was Jeffs emporium for menswear who, most importantly, took the "Provi Cheque". Heading back down Winson Green Road, on one corner was Dudley Road Junior School, after that came a row of houses which lay back from the pavements with small gardens in front of them. Next came Cuthbert Road with St. Cuthbert's Church on the corner, just before the traffic lights on the corner of Heath Street.

My mom and uncle Bill were christened at St. Cuthbert's and, for a time during the war, it was used as a temporary evacuation centre when a land mine dropped in Winson Street. Ken Storer remembers that night well as they all thought the parachute which came floating down was an enemy flier who had possible bailed out from his aircraft. But Ken's dad and his pal Jim Harris, who were in the Home Guard together, were watching as this parachute floated down. Ken's dad shouted "come on Jim, there's a ****** parachutist coming down". They both ran up the street, Ken's dad carrying his empty Sten Gun, to collar the invader when he landed. What they didn't realise was the parachute had a land mine attached to it! They came down that street faster than they went up. The people all around were evacuated to St. Cuthbert's Church hall for the night. Ken was sent down to Smethwick the following day until the land mine was made safe. Mind you this didn't stop him from going down Molliet Street over the wall and into his house to fetch his favourite toy gun.

A Mr. A. Hatton, who lived in Peel Street later on, was a regular visitor to the church hall and remembers Jack Burnett and his trio playing there every

Saturday night. The entrance fee was 2/-. St. Cuthbert's Church is no longer standing, demolished during the seventies, another well known and well loved land mark gone forever. This is now where we come back into the bottom part of Heath Street.

Heath Street looking up towards the Dudley Road possibly early 60's.
(by kind permission of Carl Chinn)

A motley crew of cheeky chappies up the top end of Heath Street
in the early 50's.
(by kind permission of J. Hill)

Chapter 3
The crossroads down to Smethwick

In the area of Heath Street in the early 1850's house building progressed in earnest. The rush to erect more and more in such a small area was becoming apparent. Forget about living standards and public hygiene, build them fast and pack them in seemed to be the objective of the land owners and the builders, and the subsequent rewards to them, were all too apparent. Freeholds and deeds would pass between parties a number of times, and of course on each passing the price would rise. In 1859 a row of back houses in Heath Street, with street facing front villas, changed hands no less than three times in the space of less than four years. In one case it all started with a Robert Seabourne who bought the lease from Thomas Newey. Seabourne, in 1856, then mortgaged it to a William Edward Simmons, and after that an agreement was made with a third man, Frederick Herbert Neville. What the first man paid for the land I haven't been able to uncover but Simmons paid Herbert £150, plus of course interest for the deeds. A comparatively small outlay which would bring in a large amount in rent monies. The bye-laws then allowed that 56 houses could be built per acre. No need of trees of gardens but just the long line of terraced houses and courts.

During the 1870's Heath Street and Winson Street were the only two readily recognisable streets in that area. In the early part of the 1880's Tudor Street, which was originally called Green Street, was built, Abberley, Dugdale, Molliet, Halberton and Grove Streets followed in quick succession. Wood Green Road and West Heath Roads came later as did Chiswell Road and Cape Street. All these streets and roads were built between the 1850's and the turn of the century, all to be filled with houses or factories. In some cases small houses were right next to the factories, no real thought given to keeping them separate. For example, in Abberley Street houses, almost all of which were back-to-back, and a couple of small shops, ran two thirds the length of the street till they came to Mapplebecks. This huge factory occupied the remainder of both sides of the street. They were metal tube drawers and the area around Abberley Street and Grove Street had the distinctive, and sometimes almost overpowering smell of suds oil and the like. I'm sure it made the outsiders wonder how the locals stood it but, like the conditions in many other parts of our city, they just got used to it. Half way along Grove Street, going off to the left, came Halbert Street, mostly factories but at the top on the corner of Dudley Road was the Cape Methodist Church. At the Dudley Road end of Grove Street was the Ionic Plating factory, and just beyond that the rear doors of the Grove Cinema.

So far we have made our way up Dudley Road, turned right at the Lea Bridge Tavern and travelled half way down Heath Street. We have visited the shops at the top end of Winson Green Road and have yet to go "down the Green". Now we carry on down the remaining part of Heath Street, where rows and rows of terraced and back-to-back houses, along with factories at the bottom, ease their way down and over the boundary into Smethwick where the road changed it's name to Cranford Street. Was Nettlefolds screw factory in Heath Street, Birmingham or Cranford Street, Smethwick? People from either side of the border would regularly argue this question out. The Grand Union Canal ran parallel with Heath Street from the Dudley Road down to Smethwick. After the junction of Winson Green Road came "the Ropery" on the banks of "the feeder". The Ropery was a colloquial name for a derelict factory which, before the war, manufactured the thinnest string, right up to the thickest tow rope, so it became known to the locals naturally as that name. A great place for adventures for the kids of the area. The "feeder" was a brick sided culvert about eight feet deep, if you discounted all the old bikes, prams and other rubbish. It's purpose was to "feed" the adjacent canal, keeping it's water up to the correct level.

More later about the locals and about certain characters who lived in Heath Street, but first let us find out where they shopped, how they lived and where the older people had a pint of beer. The small shops and other commercial premises were many and varied, let us name a few of the most well known and the ones you will readily remember. On the right hand side, opposite Tudor Street, was The Albion public house, the Ropery was immediately behind it. A few doors further down was Norris's the butchers, formerly run by Thomas Shakespeare, but what was unique in Mr. Norris's day was the fact that he made his own brand of potato crisps, not only that he cleverly turned round the spelling of his surname and called them "Sirron Crisps", an eye catching commercial idea. A little further down, still on the right hand side, we come to Alice's, a grocers shop owned and run by Mrs. Alice Smith. As Pat Dimmock, one of the locals in the 50's tells us, this was another of those small shops which, thankfully, allowed groceries "on tick". Without such shops many people would not have been able to support themselves from one week to the next. The shopkeepers weren't benevolent however, they usually added a little to the bill each week to pay for this, but Alice's and many other similar shops gave good service to the local community. Next door was another notable shop, a hardware and haberdashers owned and run by a well known character by the name of Grace Floyd, which I will tell of later on. On the left hand side of the street, just below the corner of Tudor Street was Hunt's the boot and shoe repairer. Similarly on the other side of the street, houses and shops interspersed, a florist, a confectioners and tobacconists owned by two brothers Albert and Arthur Selvey, how many of us I wonder remember the wonderful boxes of sweets and chocolates Selvey's used to make up at Christmas time. Just below that Maria Wainwright kept a greengrocer's shop.

All the houses between numbers 218 and 230 were bombed during the war and for about twelve years the land was a derelict site. Around about 1955 the city council built the public laundry and washing baths on this land. As the land between Heath Street and Tudor Street widened so the back-to-back houses became even more dense. Terraces with seven, eight and ten houses were commonplace. It was a case of put them up and pack them in. Two more grocers shops, Ashford's and Bishop's came next. On the corner of Winson Street was Bosworth's shop with a pikelet baker behind it. The smell from Bosworth's bakers was far more preferable to that from the nearby factories. Back up the street, just below Grace Floyd's there were again other yards of back-to-back houses, Dudley's followed by Lander's and Miles's yard. The correct name for this yard was Reservoir Terrace but, having the "feeder" behind it, it wasn't much like looking onto the real Edgbaston "Rezza!" These three yards alone comprised of 32 back houses. In between these yards there was a cooked meats shop which, at one time, was owned by three ladies, Elizabeth, Flora and Mary Jones. There was the Rutland Social Club at number 281, known even long after it's demise as "the coffee house". In the top house of the yard next to "the coffee house", 5/281, lived Mrs. Johnson. She was the local unofficial midwife, but it wasn't for this that she was known by the kids in the area, she made and sold toffee apples, her shop counter was a small kitchen table placed across her front doorway. Next down the street came two "chippies" within 150 yards of each other, May Owen's and Fanny Madeley's. With the Heath Street Tavern and the Queen's Arms public houses being right by, these two fish and chip shops did a roaring trade come "chucking out time". Close to the tavern was Sammy Small the bookmaker. Most working men liked a "bet" on the horses in the old days and, because it was illegal to take "bets" in those days, Sammy had a "bookie's runner" who was called Jack Taylor. Jack always stood on the corner of Heath Street and Winson Green Street, and was known as Bosworth's corner. He wore a long raincoat with deep pockets. People would slide past him and secretly pass over their "bet". On occasions Jack, the bookie's runner, would be arrested by the local bobby for taking illegal "bets" but, Sammy Small would usually be tipped off that this was about to happen and Jack would be replaced with a "stand-in" for the day. This "stand-in" would have no previous criminal record and so would only receive a small fine from the magistrate which, of course, Sammy Small would pay, and Jack Taylor would be back collecting the bets the following day. Sammy Small also owned a coach (charabanc), a splendid vehicle in blue and cream livery, but he was never a threat to Gliderway's. We kids used to be so envious on summer

10

evenings seeing the local grown-ups, dressed in their finery, boarding the coach to go on an evening run. Again below the tavern came Violet, Heath and Rose terraces containing between them 30 houses, and how many house to each lavatory? Then came Parker's Rag and Bone Merchants who were also known as scrap metal merchants well into the 1950's. Locals took their old rags there, it was another small source of income. People like Pat Dimmock and her mother even bought old heavy coats from there and cut them up to make peg or "bodge" rugs as they were also known.

The terraces right at the bottom of Heath Street, just before the city boundary, had the grand sounding names of Prince of Wales and Alton Place, but to the 28 families crammed into them and with the few available necessities of life, grand names meant nothing at all. To finish our trip down Heath Street we go back to the corner of Heath Street and Winson Street. All areas had an "uncles", this was no exception, the saviour of this area was Amy Field the pawnbroker. It was never pleasant "hocking" the old man's suit, boots or a bag of washing, but it was in many cases an absolute necessity to put some food on the table. Pawnbrokers shops were vital. Next door but one was Jackson's, a small ironmongers and electrical shop which, in later years expanded, it took over all of the pawnshop corner, and became Jackson's Bathroom Fitters, owned and run by Albert Jackson who was later to become a city councillor. After the Queens Arms public house was Challingsworth's iron foundry, then Swingler's coal and coke yard. Memories of pushing an old pram or barrow full of coke will come readily to many of the folk of the time.

We now come to the bottom of Heath Street on the left hand side, Guest, Keen and Nettlefolds, just think of the thousands who have worked there and whose livelihood depended on it.

Today almost the whole of Heath Street has been redeveloped. Semi-detached and detached houses now stand where row upon row of terraced houses stood. There are trees and front gardens with lawns and shrubs, even the kids from around there today don't need to play around "the feeder".

11

Back houses in Oxford Square, Dugdale Street.
(J. Landon)

The Bellefield Inn, Bellefield Road 1971.
(J. Landon)

Chapter 4
Never spoilt for choice

So far we have listed countless shops on our journey. From off the Winson Green Road down Heath Street and all the numerous streets that I have written about. From little hucksters to the more generous of emporiums. Only just around the corner lay a virtual ribbon of undertakings from the Lea Bridge Tavern on the corner of Heath Street right the way down Dudley Road to the Grove Cinema. A veritable bazaar for everyone. Just how did the small back street shops compete? Well they did as I have remarked on numerous times. From I suppose just being there. It would have been more handy to nip across to Mrs. so and so's, than have to traipse up onto the Dudley Road during the week.

On a Saturday morning though it would be different, and for the housewives from around the area, the main Dudley Road was the place to shop. Apart from an open market there wasn't a shop or establishment that you would be stuck for. If I were to put everyone down it would read more like a who's who and be as boring, so some I have had to miss out, others to mention, quite a few to dwell on.

The Dudley Road started from where Springhill finished. It was a continuation of the old toll road, past the hospital over the canal and railway bridges, drawing a dividing line between Brookfields and Ladywood, then again Winson Green and Edgbaston, from the factories at the top of the Springhill large and small, all mostly metal bashers. Earle and Bournes and as I've mentioned, Barker and Allens. These two were later to lose their individuality and come under the umbrella of Delta Metals. I shouldn't be talking of these as they weren't really in in Winson Green but, like St. Patricks, we'll let it become part of our area. After all a lot of our mates would have gone there. After the canal on the left hand side Edgbaston started. Not the leafy roads that were within a mile away but the tightly packed streets such as Northbrook Street, Barford Road and Icknield Port Road and so on. The Edgbaston side of Dudley Road carries on towards the Cape Hill till it shoots off smartly left and skirts M. & B.'s brewery.

Dudley Road is the dividing line between Edgbaston and Winson Green. This is a true boundary between two districts and which has, I have remarked, made its way down to Smethwick. Shops naturally dominated both sides of the road.

I'll name a few as we need to cross back over the road to 'our side'. We'll start with the Wheatsheaf pub on the corner of Icknield Port Road. Next door James Gill kept a fish and chip shop (handy for taking some home when you've had a drink). Doreen Smith the newsagents who originally came out of Lansdowne Street. Alice Bradley kept a coffee house next door to the police station, she also kept another on the corner of Bryant Street down Winson Green Road. Then came Summerfield Park. An oasis to get away to. This and the Edgbaston reservoir were the lungs to our side of the city, green grass and a vast expanse of open water. A change from playing up entries and in the horseroad. Just after the park was Bennett's the furniture shop, Rickinson a china dealer and on the corner of City Road Leslie Gabb who kept the chemists,

The Wheatsheaf on the corner of Icknield Port Road and Dudley Road.
(J. Landon)

City Road, this was the start of the posh end. A long unforgiving road if you had to walk it. Either from missing the last bus from Sandon Road (when I was courting Ed.) or as a kid spending your last bit of pocket money with your mates in Lightswood Park. The walk home never seemed to come to an end. Crossing over City Road was Lloyd's Bank this is where the difference in the two sides became very noticeable. The one side of the Dudley Road is mostly comprised of large Victorian houses. Apart from the Co-Op just past Lloyd's Bank, there wasn't another shop on that side till we went past Cavendish Road, then came the Court Steam Laundry, Livewires a television shop and next door to that was the Superb Skate Grinding Co. A bit farther down was a builders by the name of Hardeman. (I wonder if it was any relation to the ones that lived at the bottom of our entry Ed.?) and on the corner of Algernon Road Herbert Haynes kept a grocers shop. Now we are half way down Dudley Road and all that we have had is a mere handful of shops. Not until we crossed over Algernon Road did the shops congregate as far down as Shenstone Road. All these shops and the ones on the Winson Green side are taken from the 40's, 50's and into the early 60's. Perhaps many of them had been there years before. A lot though in the ensuing years were to close forever. Only the reader will know the true extent of that. Lets get back to the plot. I'll keep on the Edgbaston side of the road for the sake of our cousins on the other side. From Algernon Road we start at number 368, with the proud title of the Screw, Nut & Bolt Trade Society. What a mouthful. This must have been the Edgbaston side as there was a furriers and a gown shop. The former an A. Lewis and the latter F.C. Wright. The remainder of the shops were the same, all competing with each other down the road. Exceptions were the larger stores such as Marsh and Baxters and another Co-Op shop. The big shop on the corner of Rotten Park Road was L.M. Knight's, who had the title of "house furnishers". Another furniture shop further on down was W.H. Bright's, and it's still there today. It had an easy payment system. Many people from our area and from beyond came there for their furniture. My father-in-law bought a bedroom suite from there before the war, it was still in his house when he died in 1989. Our old chap had also purchased furniture from there and I still have the receipts to prove it. There were two coffee houses owned by Alec Douglas, both within a dozen doors of each other. They were both known as the Grove Cafe. There is a story behind this man. He brought out the popular Fleur de Lys steak and kidney pies. These were to sell in every fish and chip shop and coffee house all over the midlands. He also was the proprietor of the all night coffee stall at the bottom of Hill Street on some bombed out land just before Smallbrook Street. I think a lot of us of our age will remember this particular watering hole, when coming out of the Hippodrome or the Locarno to have a cup of coffee and something to eat before the walk back up Hill Street to get that inevitable last bus back home.

The last pub in Birmingham before the boundary is the Locomotive Engine. Why on earth it had this name I can't figure, there wasn't a railway track within a good mile, unless you count the one at M & B's brewery. There was an odd little quirk that one pub on one side of a boundary had different licensing hours from the other. The Cape of Good Hope in Smethwick at the bottom of Cape Hill, (May I add it is now a McDonalds) closed at 2.00p.m. and the Engine which is in Birmingham closed at 2.30p.m. The inevitable would happen. A mad scramble from one side of the road to the other to get that last drink in. This must have happened all along the Smethwick and Birmingham border, till the county councils got their act together and stopped the usual mad dash. We always knew where we were at that point, it was the smell of the yeast and hops from the brewery.

Now we come to the Winson Green side of Dudley Road. As I have previously written the Lea Bridge Tavern began the ribbon of shops and commercial premises stretching all the way down to the Staffordshire border. The usual shops hand in hand with each other. Some though were notable as was Jeff's the outfitters. I mentioned in my last book that it was one of those shops that took the 'Provi'. A godsend to those who could not afford the ready cash, all it needed was to save up a few bob a week, and with the help of a collector who came round to your house. Anyway lets carry on. Just after Jeff's came Duval's the butchers, practically opposite Icknield Port Road, during and after the war apart from the usual meats sold, he sold horse meat. (How many butchers shops sold it in Birmingham, and furthermore how many people would own up to buying it for themselves?) The last shop on the corner of Winson Green Road was Alex Wickets who kept a general grocers. The other side of the road is, as far as I remember, Summerfield School. Built in the 1870's and known as Dudley Road Board School. From halfway up the Winson Green Road, most of the boys and girls from the surrounding streets would have gone there, as well as those from around the Heath Street area. Just past the school on the corner of Bellfield Road, the Rt. Cecil Annette and Benjamin Dale had their consulting rooms, the former a physician and the latter a surgeon. One up from a normal doctor's surgery.

From there down to the Grove Cinema were 93 establishments! Not counting the odd pub, a couple of chapels and in 1950 the Rev. Basil N. Bentley (vicar of St. Cuthbert's) lived at 341. The other side of the road the Midland Bank had a branch there. Well known shops stood side by side with their smaller brethren. Wrenson's the grocer's, Douro wine stores. Proud sounding names such as Marshall and Knight who were milliners, Beckett of Birmingham (dyers and cleaners), Fredk. Steven the hairdressers with the up market name of the Tudor Salon. Thos. Vallender the tailor and even an antique dealer by the name of Dennis Thomas. After Heath Green Road another dyers and cleaners, Joseph Harris Ltd., Payne's the shoe repairers was next door. Lower down was the Summerfield Garage, not much of a forecourt, but a very busy place. Next door to the Trinity Methodist Chapel was William Scott's the funeral director's. Not far for the poor deceased to be moved to. Perhaps a few yards down the road George Mole, who was a fireplace merchant, worked hand in hand with his next door neighbour. Mole and Jones the building contractors. (any relation?)

Possibly one of the most well known establishments on Dudley Road was Hawley's dance hall. (The building started its life as the Dudley Road Cinema. It opened in 1912 under the management of a Mr. A. Ferguson, but closed down in 1932 when the Grove Cinema opened). From far and near dancers would make their way to this popular venue. Anybody who could dance from around the area went there. Being a dance school hundreds, possibly thousands, over the years would have been taught there. I used to go there in the back end of the 50's and early 60's. Then it was for rock and roll and the occasional smooch. This place, I'm sure, will bring back lots of happy memories to the reader. The front doors were on the Dudley Road and the building stretched down Chiswell Road. Posters adorned the outside wall informing of lessons etc. Great times, great memories. (Only now it is a snook hall, shame, Ed.)

Looking at street plans and all the businesses that were in any one area, never alone in one road. They would all make a living. Shoppers would probably go past one bakers to walk halfway down a road in preference to another. This isn't any different from today. I emphasise this as the multiples of the same sort of shops on the Dudley Road all made a living and some of these shops were practically next door to each other. In between Chiswell Road and Winson Street would have been the same type of shops as in between Winson Street and Molliet Street, and so on, but lets get back to the story.

Fishmongers were few and far between, but there was a notable one. That was Biggs'. I can remember seeing all different kinds of fish. Cod to me was with batter on, and salmon only came out of tins. The big white marble slabs abounded with plaice, cuts of hake, the silvery bluish hue from mackerel, small silvery herrings, smoked kippers, it was the place to come (excuse the pun). The shop front is still there. The name is still over the boarded up windows, but some of the wooden letters have either fallen off or, what's left of them, the paint is peeling away. Wimbush had a bakery shop, and George Mason's, the grocers also had a shop there. It said something for the road that there were so many prominent shops down there. Also a long forgotten name was Peacocks. A smaller version of Woolworth's. More of a bazaar than a Woolworth's shop would have been. Maypole Dairies had a shop next door to Robottoms the cooked meat shop. During the 50's our mom and aunts used to take their washing down to a laundrette, it was called the Bendix Home Laundry. I think it was situated where Henry Playfair the shoe shop had been. Washing would be carried in bags up the Green and down the Dudley Road. It wasn't too bad going up as the clothes were dry, but the return was harder as the wash was now wet, as there were not drying facilities in those days. It was just wash and spin, and you would have to take it home to dry. This was probably the death knell for our brew house.

The Yorkshire Grey was the last building on the corner of Winson Street. On the far corner was Moyle and Adam's. The local chemist shop was Graham Pharmacies, Dewhurst a bit lower down, with Mrs. Horton on the corner of Molliet Street who kept a fish and chip shop. A name on the far corner was one that wouldn't be forgotten. That was Harry Shotton. He was the local uncle. Nobody really wanted it to be known that they had used his pawn shop. Like a lot of similar areas it was a necessity. It meant food in your belly.

As we came down the road shops such as Blanche Barker's Off Licence and James Loon a dairyman would catch the eye. Elizabeth Bowen's milliners shop stood side by side with Churchill's the hairdresser and Austin Cook's the cooked

18

meat shop. Rosaire the florists, and on the corner of Dugdale Street a wines and spirit shop run by Gladys Conniff. On the other side on the corner of Dugdale Street was the last but one pub in Birmingham The Park Tavern (as we have already mentioned the last pub is the Engine which is on the other side of the road. Where on earth did they get these names from? The nearest one was Summerfield or the sand park at the bottom of Cranford Street).

In between the pub and the Cape Methodist Chapel on the corner of Halberton Street were a few more shops. Small now in comparison to their larger cousins further up the road but no less used. Thelma Painter kept a ladies shop, Sidney Jesson the confectioners, the Cape Paint and Hardware stores and Frank Clift the barbers. After Halberton Street Fred Aldhouse had a bike shop. Everything needed was there for when either coming out or going into the Grove Cinema a few doors down. You could get your cigs from Hickerton's on the way in, or your fish and chips from Dot Jennings on the way out, and if you had been to the matinee and wanted to cool down on a warm summer's afternoon, Polar Bear Ices were at number 469.

We have now finished our long and tiring walk down Dudley Road. We've seen all the shops on the way and those we haven't somebody else has. We are nearly at the city boundary. There is one place left. The Grove Cinema. It still stands. Not in its former glory though. At my last sighting it was a bathroom warehouse! Many a happy hour I have spent in that cinema, and so did thousands of others from the Green and Smethwick. There's no way they're going to take those memories from us.

We've made our way down towards Smethwick, now let's retrace out steps back up Dudley Road and have a walk down Winson Green Road back into Heath Street to find out about a couple of kids that grew up down that street.

Dudley Road looking towards the hospital in 1961
(J. Landon)

19

Chapter 5
Memories of a 'chap' and a 'wench' from out of Heath Street

Two of the contributors to this book were Jim Wilson and Pattie Dimmock, and even though Pattie is only about a year younger than Jim, they didn't know each other very well. Jim lived at 8/248 and Pattie at 1/243 in Heath Street. Their memories and reminiscences are strikingly similar. Their growing up in the years just after the war ran parallel with many many others who were all looking for something better in life. Unfortunately the better days would still be a way off.

Both of them remember the locality with affection. It's shops, pubs and people but, if you had a thousand people all doing the same job they would all have differing views on life. After all they are all individuals. We all have our thoughts and reasons for our actions. These two individuals are of no exception. The war had just finished and hopefully better times were to come but at this time poverty and deprivation was still lurking around most corners. So out of this comes the bond of family loyalty, and this loyalty had to be paramount. From an early age it was instilled into each child to react to family need, and if a barrow-full of coal needed to be fetched from Swingler's or a sack of coke from the gas works down Smethwick, it wasn't a case of "will you?". These chores would have to be done without question. Jim and Pattie are but two who have summed it up by saying they were proud to have come from that area but wanted something better. Happily both have achieved this ambition.

Let's start with Jim. He was born in May 1939 just five months before the start of the war. His mom and dad, Jim and Gladys, already had two children, George and Lucy. Jim wasn't to be the last, another three children followed. These were Frank, June and Audrey. The surprising thing is Jim shouldn't be here to tell his tale, as he now tells us.

"On the day I was born a very elderly neighbour came in to see me. She took one look and pressed a half-crown (12½ pence) into my tiny hand and said to my mother, 'Make the most of him, poor little thing, he's not long for this world' ". So here he is 59 years later on reminiscing over some of the happenings in his life at that time. Here now Jim recounts on his life down Heath Street.

Jim Wilson age 23 in 1962

"For what was primarily a residential street we were fortunate to have had a large number of shops, pubs and a fair number of other commercial premises, as well as the shops mentioned in other chapters. These are reminiscences of a few in particular. Our nearest grocers was Ashford's, May and Arthur. They had a large old English sheep dog called Bob. He was huge and his size and the shabbiness of his coat made him most unsuitable for a small food establishment. He seemed to have all manner of bits of stickiness attached to his long shaggy coat, bits of bacon, smatterings of butter etc. The health and safety officers would have had a high old time if it were today, but everyone loved this old dog. Like many other shops, groceries would be 'on tick'. Selected families had this privilege. At the end of the week Mom would sent one of us kids down to Ashford's to fetch the bill for that week's groceries, and on occasions there was the inevitable dispute as to what the total should be, but these were usually settled quite amicably.

Any little extra by way of money coming into the home was gratefully received and my contribution, from a part-time job, was no exception. I would rush home from school at lunch time, I was just thirteen at the time, to my part time job at the Queen's Arms public house. I had to lay the tables in the 'smoke room'. The licensees, Mr. and Mrs. Hawkins, used to serve dinners to the workers from the nearby Guest, Keen and Nettlefold screw factory. As the diners arrived Mr. Hawkins would shout the orders up to the kitchen one floor above. I would carry down about four dinners at a time on a tray and serve them to the customers. On top of this I had to help with all the washing up, eat my own dinner, and be back at school for 2.00p.m.! As if that was not hard enough, I had to go back in the evenings to prepare all the vegetables and polish all the cruets in readiness for the next day. Even this though wasn't the end of it. I also had jobs to do in the cellar, making sure it was kept spotless and all the stainless steel pipes and brass and copper fittings were all gleaming bright. There was, of course, a lighter side to my job. Davenports, who owned the pub, had strict rules that the premises should never be left totally unattended, even outside of business hours. Occasionally, on an afternoon during the school holidays, Mr. and Mrs. Hawkins would treat themselves to a trip to the pictures, either the Winson Green Picture Palace or the Grove Cinema. I would be left in charge and felt very important indeed. I probably knew more about that pub than I did about my own home. Even on a Sunday morning I would help Mr. Hawkins hose down the cream, brown and orange coloured ceramic brickwork which covered the frontage. In all it was a hard job for a young lad at that age, but I was always happy to do it, and be able to hand over a few shillings to our mom."

Growing up in Heath Street wasn't all about scrimping and saving though. The kids did have some fun too. As well as playing their various games in the street, the canal held a stranger fascination. The "ropery" and the "feeder" on the side of the canal were great magnets. As I have said the "feeder" was a deep water filled culvert, full of all sorts of unsuspecting rubbish, old bikes, prams and bedsteads. The kids, like Jim and Pattie, would try to jump across it instead of walking along to the bridge, which always seemed to be in the opposite direction to the way they wanted to go. Sometimes there would be the inevitable mishap and some unfortunate child would fall in. Thankfully there was always some kindly woman nearby who would take the child into her home and dry him off and his clothes. They were very grateful for this. If they had gone home soaking wet they would have had a good hiding no doubt.

To all of us kids the summers lasted forever and we all seemed to go to the same places, no less than Jim and his mates. The Bluebell Woods at the bottom of Hamstead Road was at that time an undeveloped and very picturesque part of Handsworth Wood. Another place was Blakeney Avenue off Lordswood Road, Harborne. But to get to these places required bus fares, and the kids would do practically anything to raise them, though the easiest way was to run an errand for a neighbour or return a beer of 'pop' bottle to the shop to retrieve the copper or two deposit off them. Jim and his mates moms would make up a parcel of 'pieces' (sandwiches for the uninitiated) and a bottle of tea and off they would go for a great day out. On high days and holidays they would be taken to the Clent Hills or the Lickeys, both exciting adventures. The former would be by Midland Red bus and the latter by tram. Staying more local though would probably mean going to the 'Rezza' or the 'sand park' just over the city boundary in Cranford Street.

Most of the younger kids from 'up the Green' were members of a club at the Grove Cinema on Dudley Road. Their addresses and other details were sent off to Warner Brothers Studios and each would be able to request photographs of their favourite film stars, and to top it all they would each receive a birthday card from Warner Brothers on the appropriate date. All very exciting for the kids who, in the main, never had two halfpennies to rub together.

After the trams finished in the 40's the buses started running down Heath Street. The B83 was 'his' route. It ran from Edmund Street in the town, down the Parade and the Sand Pits, up Spring Hill, along Dudley Road and down Heath Street and terminated at Soho in Smethwick. It's interesting to note that what would have been a good day out to Sutton Park in those days would have taken four buses to get there. Today it can be done by just one bus which runs all the way from Smethwick, through Ladywood and the city centre, on through Witton and Erdington finally reaching Sutton Coldfield and the park. Imagine what if it had been available then, those kids from out of Heath Street would have been over the moon to have been able to do this.

In the 1950's two other items of comparative luxury came to Heath Street at one and the same time. Out of an area that had been bombed during the war rose a 'Phoenix' from the ashes in the shape of the Public Washing Baths and Laundry. It had been rumoured for years that the city council were going to develop this piece of derelict land, and to everyone's surprise, it eventually came true. To a lot of housewives and mothers it meant no more scrubbing at the sink, or having to stoke the fire in a cold and miserable brewhouse. In the new public laundry each woman, for a few coppers, had her own washing machine, and a sink and scrubbing board for doing small items by hand, hot-air drying racks and electric, coin operated, ironing machines. Such luxury had never been known before. Right next door to the laundry was the washing/slipper baths. Again to most families this did away with the old tin bath in front of the fire and the fetching and carrying of buckets of hot water. Yes these washing baths were a real God send to the likes of Jim and Pittes families. Times were still very hard but small improvements like this made all the difference.

We now know something of the chap from Heath Street, his family, their shopping, the jobs he had before he left school, now the big world called him. His first job after leaving school at 15 was at a Payne's Shoe Repairers shop in Winson Green Road. Besides working on the shoe repairing he also had to travel between other branches of Payne's, taking 'work' and supplies. He salvaged a broken down delivery boy's bike and renovated it. This at least made life easier for getting back and forwards to work.

We are coming to the end of this wonderful chapter on Jim, the man it was thought would never be reared. Jim himself believes that although life in Heath Street was hard and at times difficult, it stood him and others in good stead for the future, preparing them for later on and helping them to make a better life for themselves.

Let's now look at the wench that came out of the same street.

Chapter 6
A tale to tell

Her name now is Pat Smith. It used to be Dimmock before she married. I pick this lady out as she was my first inspiration for this book. No different to lots of other girls from that time, but her story touched me. I will now put it in Pat's words.

"I had a somewhat complicated start if life. When I was fifteen years old I learned that Rose and Arthur Dimmock, who raised me as a child, and whom I called mom and dad, were in fact my grandparents. Though not maternal I still class them as such. I was born in 1940 and my mother was, in reality, my big sister. I never did find out who my real father was. My birth was just another wartime statistic. My real mom was at the Mission of Hope in the Fulham Road, London. She was there as a homeless child.

"Arthur and Rose Dimmock unfortunately could never have any of their own children. So in those early days they adopted them. Children were taken into care by the 'Mission' and were passed on to suitable parents. There were three others that were taken on before my mom. They were May, Gordon and Lizzie. I never knew these though. My mom was adopted in 1919. I still have the original receipt from the 'Mission'. It reads "I give this child Myrtle Helen Claridge in keeping with the sum of 10/-". This was a one and only payment. My real mom seemed to remember that her parents had come from the U.S.A. and left her at the 'Mission'. You may ask why London? Well Arthur was a Royal Marine and based at Chatham. After he wed Rose they went to live in married quarters.

"This was probably in the early part of the 20th century. After many years in the marines he left the services and they came to live in Birmingham. During the early 30's they lodged with a Mr. and Mrs. Harbage and eventually moved into 1/243 and that is where I came into the picture.

"We lived in a back house, up a dark entry, in Heath Street. The top of the entry opened into a yard containing two houses, ours and one other which was used for a 'lock-up', a storage used by the woman who owned the houses, Grace Floyd. Grace Floyd was the 'definite eccentric' who owned several premises in Heath Street. She lived alone with her three dogs, Johnnie a massive Alsation, Flash a giant Greyhound and Billy a black and white mongrel. She also kept

Pattie Dimmock in her gran's house in the 1940's

ducks and chickens in some of the empty houses and outhouses. One of her unoccupied houses was full of haberdashery items and boxes and boxes of shoes. Among this assortment of items there was a blunderbuss, several bayonets and swords. Where these came from I never found out but I remember I used to make a copper or two by sneaking my school friends into the house and charging them a penny each to see them. Our mom used to pay Grace Floyd 13/- a week to rent their house and to help find this rent money she used to collect the fees from people who rented parking spaces on a piece of Gracie's land, down at the bottom of Heath Street by Nettlefold's. It had gates to secure it and our mom had the job of locking the gates after dark. Even though Gracie was an eccentric my parents never had a bad word to say about her, as they used to say "she was a golden woman, without her we might well have gone under". At the canal end of the yard there were derelict out-buildings which were probably used as workshops at one time. Our house had no running water, this had to be carried from a stand-pipe in the yard. The water was kept in a large jug on the kitchen table. Cooking was done on the old black-leaded cooking range. The house didn't have electricity and the lighting was by gas. To keep food chilled it stood on a marble slab in the cellar. Most people kept their coal in the cellar, we didn't, ours was kept in a cubby hole off the kitchen where we also stored the coke. Our house was literally full of antiques as Rose and Arthur Dimmock, my mom and dad (grandparents), were antique dealers at one time. In the living room we had a huge rocking horse that dad got from a fairground carousel. There was a huge dresser with big wide drawers. It was decked with salt glazed plates and lots of china which had a blue 'crossed-guns' trade mark, which I now know to be Meissen. All very collectable indeed. A beautiful white dinner set with green spots which I believe was Royal Doulton, many Toby Jugs and lots of cigar tins which my dad had brought back from all around the world when he was serving with the marines. There were also three miniature Buddas made from ivory. All these fine things sadly disappeared before I was much older.

"There was a drain which ran down the middle of our yard and, after a fall of rain, it would flood out into a pool over the yard. No wonder the kids were

25

forever going down with coughs, colds, chronic bronchitis and even diphtheria. Our playground was the streets. Hopscotch, skipping ropes etc. all the games that kids could play on the pavement. Not very far away, just over the boundary in Cranford Street was the 'sand-park', not much of a park really, more a recreation ground with a few swings and roundabouts, but it did have a small sand-pit for the younger children to play in. This park was renowned throughout the area and we would play there for hours.

"As I have said along the back of our house ran the canal and us kids would play along the banks. The canal ran alongside Nettlefolds. As kids we would fish with nets for sticklebacks that we knew as 'Jackbannacks'. Barges full of coal were frequent, and during the late summer me and our mom would pick buckets of blackberries. This was our bit of insurance for the winter months ahead. We would trade blackberries for coal with the 'Bargees' and occasionally the odd bodge rug. We would use any bag that we could muster. More often than not it was to be brown paper carriers.

"I regret nothing except that I wish Arthur and Rose Dimmock could have witnessed me in later years as a successful auctioneer."

Pattie Dimmock in her teenage years.
(by kind permission of Pattie Smith)

Chapter 7
The big move on the handcart up the Green

In 1934 the big move was on. Ken's dad had hired a hand cart. They were moving up in the world. Well I say up, if you can call going 'UP' the Green as being the right word. Ken Storer and his family lived in a back-house in Wellington Street. This was a move upwards as far as Ken's mom and dad were concerned. They were living in a back to back. Now they were to reside in another back-house but this one had a back yard and a front garden, though they had to share four outside 'lavies' and two brewhouses with six other families! It took several trips to move all of their worldly possessions. Ken remembers going along with his dad on one of the journeys/ Up the Green over the railway and canal bridges, down Heath Street into Tudor Street, finally arriving at 2/82 Winson Street at which their yard faced the end of Tudor Street. A high wall at the back separated them from the houses in Molliet Street. So today we could have said that they were self-contained! They had a small garden in the front and Ken's dad built a rabbit hutch there. Later on an Anderson shelter was put next to it. Shows how much you can put into a small garden.

Of all the neighbours that he can remember in this small enclave were a Mr. and Mrs. Harris and a Mrs. Guest and her unmarried daughter Ada who lived next door to them. In front of his house on the street was Perry's the greengrocers. This shop was really old fashioned by today's standards. Soaked peas, potatoes in urden sacks and all covered in mud. (Quarter pound of mud for every pound of potatoes!) Close by was a shop that used to sell bits of groceries, firewood etc., and the proverbial cigs. Mind you this one had a cigarette machine on the wall outside, where he thinks for a penny two cigarettes and two matches tied in an elastic band could be got.

At the top end of the street was, or still is, the Yorkshire Grey public house. (Mr. and Mrs. Dix who lived down by the Bamfords in Wellington Street went to live up there in the 50's, another family that left our end. Strange, there must have been an attraction of some sorts. Ed.) The cockle man could be seen selling his shellfish, serving from a pint pot, outside the pubs. That man must have had muscles on his muscles. All the folks from that area remember seeing his cart outside all of the hostelries. To pull that hand cart in such a short time around the district at lunchtime must have been quite a feat.

Just below the pub on the opposite side was a cobblers shop. Ken doesn't remember the name of the owner but remembers boots, the soles facing outwards, showing pictures of dogs and ships picked out in shoe rivets and coloured in leather dyes. Further down the road opposite Cape Street was the Bellefield Garage and the Bellefield Inn. To come away from this part for a moment Ken remembered one of his favourite places. Just below Tudor Street was a shop that was run by a Mr. Standing. He dealt in second hand comics and books. When Ken was growing up during the war, he used to swap his Hotspurs, Adventures and Champions there. (I bet he wished he'd have kept them!) If you took two back you would get one in exchange. Otherwise they cost you a penny. New ones twopence. But lets get back to the story. Across the road was the double knack to Molliet Street. He used to ride his bike through it and get a good cussing off from any one that was walking through from the other direction. There was a little shop up the road from his yard kept by a Mrs. Salt, but you know for the life he can't remember what she sold! Before the days of the wine cellars and drinks cabins, were the off-licences, or better known as outdoors. Up until the late 1950's a lot of us kids would fetch their elders beer either in a jug or a bottle. Ken would fetch his dad's beer in a bottle. A paper seal was put over the stopper. That way it would be legal to serve to children under-age. I presume we all did it, and no doubt we all had a taste on the way home.

On the corner of Abberley Street was the general store Ken's mom used mostly. It was a Mrs. Hand's who kept it. Anything about shopping was a bore for a young lad, but Mrs. Hand's sold halfpenny bars of Cadbury's chocolate. That shop he was never to forget.

As he grew up so the errands would come his way. One was fetching coal in a hired barrow from Swingler's in Heath Street. His reward, the deposit from the barrow!

His dad worked at John Wilkes and Mappleback's. Unfortunately living close to work would bring disaster. During the war the area was heavily bombed. There were so many targets to hit. It didn't matter if civilians were caught up in the action. The houses in the vicinity of Ken's had all their windows blow out when a bomb dropped in Molliet Street. There was even a direct hit on an Anderson shelter in Cape Street. If nothing else it brought out a spirit of invincibility in people. No more than young Ken. He had no fear of the air raids. He felt it couldn't happen to him or his family. He had been evacuated to Worcester at the outbreak of war, but came home at Christmas 1939 and never went back. He once walked home from the first house at the Grove Cinema in the middle of a raid. The sound of the Ack-Ack guns echoed up the entries in the street with a flat banging sound. Shrapnel was rattling across the roof tops and yet the fear of it all didn't worry him.

The war over and after leaving Dudley Road School Ken went onto George

Dixon's the grammar school in City Road. This now was all about growing up. Even though at thirteen he still wore short trousers, his pal Sammy Feeney, from Tudor Street, lent him a pair of long ones. Sammy's dad sneaked him into the Grove to see his first 'H' film. It was Frankenstein. He was most disappointed. Instead of being frightened it was a let down. Perhaps going through a war had made him hard. Certainly a bloke with a bolt through his neck didn't put any fear into him. He now lives in West Heath and is now a remarkable artist. He drew the pictures for the cover of my first book. I'm pleased to know him. Although he lives across the other side of the city his heart, I am sure, will always be on ours.

Chapter 8
Parliament Square? Why not!

There wasn't an area called Parliament Square but there might well have been due to the many streets named after the members of Lord Aberdeen's government of 1852-1855. Maybe it needed something a bit more grand sounding to 'lift' the area after the notorious workhouse was built in 1851. The streets to the west of the workhouse and the hospital were built no different to the other streets around but with grander names, Aberdeen, Lansdowne, Carlisle and Peel streets and of course Norman Street, the odd name out. The city fathers didn't yet know of a Lamont! Aberdeen street ran from Dudley Road, skirting the grounds of the future City Hospital, and on down to Winson Green Road. Lansdowne Street went off Aberdeen Street and was a cul-de-sac due to the canal being at the end of the street. It did, however, cross two other streets, Peel and Carlisle Streets. The one remaining, Norman Street ran off Carlisle Street. The first 100 yards or so of Aberdeen Street was taken up by Dudley Road Hospital. Sidney Flint, another contributor to this book, remembers his family moving here in the 1930's from Ladywood. When the slum clearance began they found Aberdeen Street a great improvement to where they had lived previously. But even though this house had two living rooms, two bedrooms and a cellar, they still didn't have a bathroom, and had to share an outside lavatory with several other families. Their front or 'best' room was at the back of the house and looked out over the railway line and the canal. At the time of the outbreak of the war Sidney Flint can only recall two shops in the entire length of Aberdeen Street, three if you include Bryant's furniture shop right at the bottom on the corner of Winson Green Road. One of the shops was a general store owned by Mr. Jenns, the other was a fruit and vegetable shop owned by Mr. and Mrs. Stringer. Mr. Stringer was also the local penny wink man. He toured all the pubs in the area, and had the occasional half pint along the way. Although Mr. Stringer could usually, and more often than not, be found in the Queen's Head public house opposite his shop, the shop at this time being managed by a Mrs. Wilson. Thankfully the residents of the 'square' didn't have too much in the way of major bombings. Though there was one major attack when direct hits went in a pattern. One dropped at the end of Carlisle Street, one missed Peel Street, another one dropped at the end of Aberdeen Street, then missed the Dudley Road and the final one dropped in

Coplow Street. The rest of Aberdeen Street didn't suffer too much along with Lansdowne Street. Incendiary bombs were the biggest threat and most of the streets had their fire watchers and numerous sand bags and stirrup pumps. The bottom of Aberdeen Street did suffer first and this one particular night bombs began to drop further up the street which was on Sidney Flint's area who was at that time a fire watcher. He remembers looking around for his helpmates, they were nowhere to be seen. Women came out of the air-raid shelters to help him pump the water. Later, when things had quietened down, his neighbour and helpmate told him proudly. "I've helped to put out thirty bombs down the street". His heart then sank like a lead balloon when Sidney told him that one of the fires they hadn't been able to extinguish was the one that came through *his* roof. It had gone through the tiles and ceiling and was burning a hole in his bedroom floor! His wife had to come out from the shelter to help fight the fire. The poor chap was not allowed to forget that night in a hurry.

There were happier times in Aberdeen Street and amateur dramatics played their part. Who remembers George Hill who ran the 'October Players', and who had their rehearsal rooms in stables at the back of his house? Perhaps there are still a few Winson Green-ite thespians treading the boards who started with this society.

After the war Sidney Flint remembers buying a bedroom suite from Bryant's the furnishers. Solid American Mahogany and with the statutory 'utility mark' on each piece. To this day he still uses the 'tallboy' as a piece of office furniture, much to his wife's disdain, she wants it thrown out.

Dave Avery was a local lad and remembers his youth in that area. Like us all he was familiar with his local street. More of a couple I suppose than all of them, but he gave me the utmost of help with the rest of the streets.

Now we're going to make our way from the other end, turning into Norman Street off the Winson Green Road. Mixed in between terraced houses was the usual general provisions store, sounds posh, but it was the little local grocer, selling anything from fire lighters to the weeks grocery. People could have gone round the corner and up the Green to do their shopping, but they couldn't have had their bit of tick from the Co-Op! Mrs. Wooley's was the first then followed a few yards along by Florrie Lamb's. On the other side of the street was Mrs. Moore's fish and chip shop. Dave Avery could always get a free bag of chips for taking her a load of newspapers. Fish and chips have never tasted the same! It had to change though, you never knew where the papers had been. Down at the very end of Norman Street was the council yard. When Dave was a lad he remembers horse drawn carts and original steam rollers trundling out of the gates. The yard was also serviced from the canal which ran alongside the back of the yard. As I said earlier, this was the scene of the first hit of the bombs as they came across the prison and canal. Then came Mrs. Wooley who kept the shop just down the street. Her son went into business after the war selling ex-American army lorries. Sounds vaguely familiar to Bushells out of Lodge Road. Still I suppose this was going on all over the country at that time. Norman Street at this point ran down to the hospital wall as a cul-de-sac. (I can't think of any other part of Winson Green as having dead ends in four streets side by side all ending at the same wall).

Round the corner came Carlisle Street where Dave's gran lived. Opposite her house was a yard up a narrow alley owned by Shell-Mex. Dave remembers this well as occasionally lorries would have a hell of a game to reverse out onto the road and would have to back over towards his gran's house. On a couple of occasions a lorry would come too far over and reverse into his gran's house. Not that much damage was ever done, but it has always stuck in his memory. Another thing that he never forgot was the frosted glass in his gran's house. After the bombing the landlord must have run out of clear glass and so it was frosted glass for as long as he recalls. Next to his gran's were the 'new houses'. They had been built over an old coal yard. (There must have been plenty of slack in their back gardens.) We have missed one particular oasis out. It was the Cottage of Content on the corner of Norman Street and Carlisle Street. Not a very big pub but a popular one.

Well we've had our half pint in there so lets move back up the street. Next door was Clal Roses another general provision shop. Up the street lived a local character, if you could say it that way. His name was Ted Ball. He worked at McKecknies and would hold his four square bible meetings during his lunch hour. Apart from yet another shop owned by a Mrs. Houghton there were no other shops in Carlisle Street. Now we'll start to make our way towards the Dudley Road via Lansdown Street. There weren't a lot of shops, but what there was were well used and known in that small area. Minnie Allen kept a shop, as usual selling everything. Her brother was the local insurance agent. He was noted for his rather large and somewhat old sit up and beg bike. Next door was Mrs. Hind's a paper shop. When her husband died she later remarried a Mr. Andrews, and the name changed over the door. It was to change again when a Doreen Gilbert, later Smith, took it over. Later on she went up in the world and opened a double fronted newsagents next to the police station on Dudley Road next to Summerfield Park. Doreen's mom kept a little shop on the other side of the street from the Hind's, another general shop, but was renowned for her home-made faggots and peas. Next to come was the cul-de-sac which was known as Little Peel Street. Dave's aunt lived in one of the two rows of houses, one called the Laurels and the other the Poplars. She played the organ at the little chapel in Peel Street and her daughter, Margaret, also taught Sunday school there.

The street mostly consisted of houses. I suppose there were enough shops anyway. This wasn't the case as a Mrs. Gibson kept a shop and even employed an assistant. Dave Avery, like all of us from these sort of neighbourhood,s wondered how they all made a living. Well they did, hand to mouth at times possibly, but they got by. Above was a builder by the name of Barrett's. Mr. Needham was the foreman, and used to live on the site. He was, as Dave remembers, quite high up in the Salvation Army.

On the corner of Aberdeen Street and Lansdowne Street was the welfare. Many a poor, sickly bab would have been brought there, and if too poorly sent round the corner to the hospital. But here they would have been weighed and checked and after the war would have been given that wonderful elixir of life, orange juice. During the 1950's there was a polio scare. This was to be a central immunisation centre for the Green. (Even though I came from down the bottom end of Winson Green I was taken up with my mom to the welfare of an inoculation ed.) During this time Dave's dad had a bad attack of the gout. His doctor wouldn't take any chances, and he was admitted into hospital. Anyway lets turn ourselves around and make our way back towards Peel Street. On the corner was the Oak public house kept at that time by a Mr. and Mrs. Baker. When as lads Dave and his mate would climb the wall at the back, help themselves to a few empties, climb back over and take them around the front to the outdoor. He seems to think that they were the only ones, I bet they weren't.

Now we are in Peel Street. Next door to the pub was Mrs. Girdons another local shop. He was now on his own patch, and names spring out at him. Mrs. Bragg, Mr. and Mrs. Harris and their three sons Alfred, David and Jimmy. Next to these was their little shop, really a converted house made into a haberdashery and tobacconists, but I'll come back to this as it warrants a bit more on the Avery story. The names of the Evans', Gibbs and Waterhouse's spring to mind. Even a man by the name of Charlie Cattermole who kept large dogs. Ferocious look, but harmless, but they still put the frighteners into Dave. Below were the gardens. They were called this as they were the only houses in the area to have the gardens in the front instead of at the back. There were four houses in total. Pretty unique in those days. Then came the Sir Robert Peel, an Atkinson house run by a Mr. and Mrs. Alf Summerfield (my sister-in-laws late parents Ed.) Up the back entry was Bernard Row the local decorator. Now here's a strange thing which certainly wouldn't be seen today. Right opposite the Peel was a shop that was kept by a Mr. and Mrs. Williamson. Prior to bonfire night they would sell, as many others did, fireworks, but they had them stacked up outside! None would be touched or stolen. They would be put out in the morning when dry, and taken back in if it rained or at night. The mind boggles to think of that happening today. Down below was another general shop owned by a Mrs. Foresbrook but with a difference. It was the only shop in the area by the name of Waldron, another sweet shop, where you could have bought Lyons three colour ice-cream. (Dave spoke about the Griffin family. Two lads and three girls, they say a small world, and it was, as I was in the Boy's Brigade with one of the lads by the name of Barry). I spoke of the chapel which Dave's aunt went to. This would now be classed as a centre, as in those days silent films would be shown at the grand price of three pence. Not a sign yet of the multiplex cinemas. Mrs. Walker who was the caretaker lived close by there. All streets had some sort of character. The one down there was a man by the name of Ted Pritchard, known as 'big Ted'. He certainly was. He was around 20 stone, but a big friendly character. He lodged in Peel Street and worked as a porter down the fish market, and as often as not would bring a nice bit of fish from work. All the kids knew him, and was well liked. Being a Brummie supporter helped.

There were other shops in the street, amongst them were two paper shops practically side by side, Heath's and Barnett's, but others Dave has forgotten their names as the years have gone on. We now have come to the end of the 'Square' as such, and have come to the Smith's Arms. Not too great an area but finding out a little bit more of my precious Green has fascinated me.

Let's now make our way from the L.M.S. railway station on the Winson Green Road right the way down and bring back some more memories.

In the bar of the Sir Robert Peel in Peel Street.
(Author)

34

*The corner of Aberdeen Street and Winson Green Road, note the sign on the
side of Ward's shop for the sale of loose port at 4/6 a pint.
(J. Landon)*

*The Queen's Head, Aberdeen Street.
(This is the only building still standing there today)
(J. Landon)*

Aberdeen Street in 1962 showing the houses 125 to 132
before re-development.
(J. Landon)

A yard at the rear of number 40 Aberdeen Street, note the passage way to
more back houses, just prior to demolition in the 70's.
(J. Landon)

36

Chapter 9
Nannie Dacey

Jennie's gran lived all her life in Aberdeen Street. Her name was Rose, she lived in a terraced house no different to the others up and down the street, but to Jennie it was a home like no other. She would go to her nans to do the weekly chore of cleaning the hallway. Jennie would wet-mop and then dry the floor tiles, then, with great relish, would polish them to a high shine. There were reds of all hues and creams with black outlines. After this job was finished in her own personal way she would pretend that this was her own little private house. Only the thought that she would have to do the same job again at her own home would bring her back down to earth. Like lots of people at that time

Rose was always strapped for a few bob during the week and would send Jennie down Peel Street to a money-lender. This fellow was no fat cat with a silver watch chain and a big cigar, just the opposite. He lived in a back house up an entry. He would be sat in the doorway with his shirt sleeves rolled up, a collarless shirt, round wire-rimmed spectacles and the proverbial flat cap. Jennie would tell him how much her nan wanted, it might have been just a couple of bob. He would lick the end of his stub of a pencil, out would come his little dog-eared book and he would write down the date and how much money had been borrowed. No words were exchanged. He would go into the house and come back handing over the amount asked for, off Jennie would skip back to her nans to give her the money, with never a thought of how nan would every pay it back, and at how much commission!

Jenny Hall dressed up for
Coronation day
(by kind permission of J. Hall)

37

Chapter 10
Anne's Memories

" Moving house wasn't any great hardship. It was only from one end of Icknield Port Road to the other so to speak. We lived on Monument Road opposite the swimming baths. We kept a hairdressers, and we lived over the shop. Next door to us was the post office, and the owners, Mr. Moorhouse and Mrs. Bates, were our landlords. In 1944 they helped us to move to the Green. This was all due to the bombing. Previously we had lived in Cavendish Road, so we knew our way round a little.

"We moved on a wonderful hot summer's day in June. Dad had come home from the Merchant Navy on leave. I was made aware to make myself scarce. So I read a book and duly kept out of the way!

"The house was number 34 on Winson Green Road. When looking out from the front door, I was delighted, right opposite was a fish and chip shop. Twice a week after that I was sent over for two 10 penny fish and two four pennorth of chips. I knew I was going to like living in Winson Green.

"This was now 1944 and we still had a shelter. Not one of the concrete types or the Anderson but a Morrison. One of those which in turn was used as a table. All steel. A pity though if the house collapsed around you. A year later, on another wonderful summers day, the end of the second world war was declared and the celebrations started.

"The day after the announcement was made a street party was held in Bellefield Road, just round the corner. Well we couldn't really have had a party in our road, could we? It was too busy with traffic! Dad had once again come home on leave, which made the day even better for me and our mom. Everyone went completely mad from 2.00 in the afternoon when the tea was laid out for the kids on tables in the middle of the road. From one house to another pianos were brought out. This was going to be the best sing-song ever. Bonfires were lit in the streets. Later on in the evening, with great reluctance, we kids were put to bed, but we all knew that the party never finished till the next morning.

"In September of that year I started at George Dixon's Grammar School in City Road where I met a girl by the name of Iona Jones who was to be a close friend for many years to come. She lived at the far end of Cuthbert Road. One day she suggested would I like to go with her to the Children's Evening Service in

St. Cuthbert's church hall. I think it was run by the Youth for Christ organisation and they attracted the kids from around the area like bees to the honeypot. It was always packed out. The hymn-singing was very jolly, no miserable tunes and a story which we could all relate to. It was there that I met this great young man. His name was Reggie Bourne and he lived in what were known as the 'cottages' situated at 14/47 Cuthbert Road. He came to the services with his mates, Bobby Brookes, Billy Webb and Raymond Hadley. Billy Webb lived in Heath Street on the right hand side going up towards the Dudley Road and I remember a friend of mine was madly in love with him. I don't think I should mention her name though as it was a long time ago. But if she reads this she'll remember. To get back to the story. All of us knew of the Rice sisters and their shop on the corner of Northbrook Street. One day Reggie turned up at one of the evening services in a very smart outfit, a blue sports jacket and grey trousers, he looked the bees knees. It was rumoured that Miss Rice had provided them. It appeared that she often, probably with the aid of the church funds, kitted out the poorer kids from the neighbourhood from her little shop. At the time of the harvest festival we would take all the food gathered to a home for ex-prisoners down Winson Green Road.

"Reg's dad, Bill, worked as a bookie's runner for Sammy Small in Heath Street but I didn't know much about it at the time. A grandfather of his lived at number 47, and though Reg and his sisters used to call him by that title till he passed away, he always found that the old fellow was a bit offish. What they didn't know was that he was really their great uncle. Their real grandfather had died in the first world war, and nobody had told them any different! Reg never found out till many years later.

"What I really remember most about Winson Green was the kindness and friendliness of everyone there, the shopkeepers and even the policemen at the station next to Summerfield Park. The park itself was a lovely place. The flowers, I remember, were so magnificent especially after the war. I must have been around ten in 1945 when I helped myself to some flowers to take home to mom from out of the park. Unfortunately the 'parkie' caught me and asked for my name and address. I gave it to him and on the same evening the 'parkie' came to our house. I was upstairs in bed. He told mom what had happened and mom had to give him five shillings for my sins of picking the flowers, (even though he had confiscated them). Did I get a good slap the next morning. I never did that again. Flowers in the future came from Evans' shop on the other side of the road, more expensive but less painful.

"We could walk down Heath Street or Cuthbert Road after dark, it was always quiet and safe. I can never remember anyone being robbed or molested. It was unheard of. (Perhaps it was because most of the men were still on active service and possibly because films which were shown then were not as violent as they are now).

"In December 1949 after living 'down the Green' my parents bought a semi in Harborne because they said that Winson Green was very common! and I would meet 'nicer people' in our new district. Admittedly Harborne, in my youth, was a lovely place, it always seemed to me it hadn't got the friendliness of the 'Green'. People in Winson Green didn't *pretend*, what you saw, was what you got. I was very unhappy for along time after we left Winson Green. We didn't have a car and I was told that on 'pain of death' that under no circumstances was I to go back there, with one exception, they allowed me to go the Christmas party at the church hall.

"One day in 1954 I got off my bus in Steelhouse Lane to go my job at the Council House and Reggie Bourne was riding his bike behind my bus. So my mother's plans to meet someone posh in Harborne failed.

"We've now been married for 40 odd years and two children and four grandchildren later we have never forgotten our times from down the 'Green'. (To paraphrase a saying from a great Brummie, "you can take the kid away from the Green, but you can't take the Green away from the kid, Ed.)

The Boys Brigade Band from the 39th. at an anniversary march from
St. Cuthberts in the early 50's.
(by kind permission of Anne Bourne)

40

Chapter 11
G.K.N. an employer too many

The name that was on everybody's lips from the top of the Green and beyond. Not now, it's great former self is finished. Now there is just the name of Nettlefolds over the existing building. In the late eighties the company that was left, sold out to European Industrial Services Ltd. and another of Birmingham's once great factories declined. Guest Keen's were the largest employer's from that area. Heath Street reverberated to the amount of people that made their way to these works. It was the cornerstone of employment to many thousands of workers over the years. Unlike today the saying went "keep your nose clean son, there's a job for life at Guest Keen's". This wasn't the way unfortunately. Greater imports of the same type of manufacturing eventually made the 'job for life' less promising. During the period after the war and up to the 1970's it seemed that it would go on for ever, but that wasn't to be.

Generations would pass through those gates. From young women working on a press (my mom worked there till she got married) to young lads serving an apprenticeship and older men using their particular knowledge of the trade. This was the firm to work for. It provided for hundreds of families and may I add the shops and pubs in the area. Let us now find out a little bit more of this once huge factory in Heath Street.

The story starts with Joseph Nettlefold a manufacturer of screws. In 1854 he was jointed by his nephew Joseph Chamberlain who came from London at the tender age of eighteen. This was to be a very successful partnership. The name duly changed to Nettlefold and Chamberlain. There was also an amalgamation with another large company, The Patent Nut and Bolt Co. Ltd., situated at the London Works in Smethwick. This would prove to be one of the largest manufacturers of screws in the country. The firm grew in size on the borders of Staffordshire and Warwickshire, occupying a sizeable portion of land at the end of Heath Street and the beginning of Cranford Street. New automatic machines acquired from Germany enabled screws to be mass produced, instead of being hand made which up until this time they had been. (A second factory was built in Stirchley next to the inevitable canal in the 1850's.)

Joseph Chamberlain went on to become a Birmingham councillor and later Lord Mayor. His style and foresight changed Birmingham out of all proportion. Dragging and kicking, he and other notable people made our town into a second city, but this is another story.

Later on towards the turn of the century the name of Chamberlain was dropped and the names of Guest and Keen were added to Nettlefold's. This was to be, as I've said, the largest of the factories in the area and to people like Ivor Havins was their workplace.

Ivor Havin checking his work at G.K.N. in Heath Street.
(by kind permission of Ivor Havin)

Ivor had no idea what he wanted to do when his schooldays were over. He had no thoughts of what kind of job he would take. It seemed the most obvious of work places to go to was G.K.N's. As both of his parents worked there, along with his grandma and a few aunts and uncles along the way, there was only one question, would they have him? Well they did, and after a long summer holiday, with not the faintest thought to the future he began his working life in that huge factory in Heath Street. It made sense though, living in Woodland Street he could fall out of bed and into work in no time. Although this wasn't always the case. The 'bull' (a loud hooter) would sound around the area at 7.30

42

a.m., it couldn't be missed. (every large factory would have their own distinctive hooter). This was the last but one warning to get into work on time. The gate commissioners were very strict. Employers would have to be through the gates by the 7.45 bull. Ivor, at times, would just squeeze through the gates as the last bull went off. Anyone after that would be locked out, and half a day's pay would be lost. To a mere lad of fifteen in the early days of September 1952 it was awesome. From being a schoolboy and coming into what we call the real world, would need somebody to help and bring him into his new surroundings. This man who was to be his first foreman was Jack Smith, he took him to Harold Ashton who was a fitter on the shop floor, and who would be in charge of Ivor and other trainees for the next few months. After, he would decide what jobs Ivor would be taught whilst under his wing. Ivor was taught how to dismantle different parts of a machine, and what to keep and what to dump as scrap.

The first two weeks went by and he received his first wage packet, owing to the fact that he had to work a week in hand, Ivor picked up the grand total of £3.9.9. The money didn't last long and to this day he has still got that first wage packet. (no money, just the packet). A rise was given every year, normally on a birthday, the grand sum of 10/- (50p) per week.

After leaving Harold Ashton he was sent to another instructor, he was taught how to build and repair the spindles that were used on the C11 worming machines. These machines cut woodscrews by running a cutter along the blank while it was spinning in the spindle. At this time he was with Bill Whitstance. Ivor stopped with him for about two years. Then the inevitable happened, he received his call up papers to do his National Service.

From 1956 to 1958 he served in the Royal Engineers. He received basic training at Malvern then went to Aldershot. Then, as a driver of just three and a half hours of instruction, he was posted to Minden in Germany. At this time the Suez Canal crisis reared its ugly head. Ivor had been transferred to another base in Germany. As reservists were brought in from the U.K. all of the vehicles were put on stand-by. Ivor was then transferred to the Regimental Police Staff. He liked this new position and applied to join the R.M.P. but was told he would have to sign on for another five years. He liked the job but didn't fancy spending another five years at it. He was demobbed in January 1958. This was to be a memorable year as it turned out. Ivor met Pauline (a Winson Green wench who came from out of Crabtree Road) in the August, they got engaged just a fortnight later and married within the next 14 weeks. People probably got the wrong end of the stick and said it wouldn't work, but they both proved them wrong and celebrated their 40th wedding anniversary in 1998.

On being demobbed, Ivor returned to his old job only to find there was no future in woodscrews being made in the way which he remembered before his call-up. The method taken up in cutting a screw was all time consuming on a machine known as a C11. With a newer generation of machine, the C11

43

became obsolete. It was now back to training school. He was to learn to operate newer types of machines, and became a heading setter. This would involve running coils of wire through the machine to be forged into blanks ready to be roll threaded. Ivor worked on a number of headers till his redundancy in the late 80's. This, he feels, was due to the amount of screws being made in the far east, and their low price which was far less than they could be made for in this country.

The friends Ivor made over the years at G.K.N. were all long term friendships. He never met anyone there that he wouldn't have invited to his home. Ivor feels that to mention some, would mean to forget others, and feels this is a tribute to all of his workmates.

Like a good many of the large factories in Birmingham with a thought for their workers' well-being, G.K.N. has its own medical centre on site. The centre was rumoured, at the time, to have cost in the region of £250,000 to bring it up to date. There were doctors, nurses and even its own chiropodist (with an apt name of Miss Treadwell!). During the 50's there was a doctor by the name of Lloyd, his daughter Sue Lloyd, an actress, was to be more renowned, but to the workers, less important to the well being of the factory. Ivor and other trainees up to the age of 18 had to have regular check-ups. Even though the factory was only a stone's throw from Dudley Road Hospital it could accommodate any emergency.

The company even used to lay trains on during the annual holiday prior to the last war. It would take their employers to the seaside. This was before Ivor worked there, but the feeling of a family company had been established.

As I said at the beginning of the chapter the company in the late 1980's was scaled down to a mere fraction of its former self, but to the many who timed their clocks to the sound of the 'bull', this factory would never be forgotten at the bottom end of Heath Street.

Chapter 12
To the bottom of the Green

After crossing over the canal and railway bridges, Winson Green Road now became known as the bottom end of the Green. It still had the same multifarious amount of shops, each with their own distinctive appeal. On the left hand side was a name that said all at that time in the re-moulding of Birmingham, it was Greaves the builders. The elder Mr. Greaves gave his name to his son to promote, and did he. Huge developments across the city began to rise with this name on the bill boards. In later years it died away, but that was where it all started from. Next to him was Bradley's coffee house on the corner of Bryant Street, as I've remarked, Mrs. Bradley had another one on the Dudley Road.

On the other side of the road just below the old Winson Green railway station was Adams's the sweet shop. After the war when sugar was still on ration, local kids took their sugar into this shop whereupon he would make you up a big bag of sucks. Next door was a tobacconist by name of Troy's. Going down the Green at this point Aberdeen Street is to the right and Bryant Street to the left. Bryant Street runs alongside the railway then into Clinton Street and at the end turns a right angle into Magdala Street. In between Bryant and Magdala runs Blackford Street, possibly one of the few spots of the Green that wasn't knocked down. The area was built before the turn of the century, and guess what, not a shop in sight in any of these four streets! The only business was a bedding manufacturer by the name of Bryant's at the end of Clinton Street. These streets though were renowned by a lot of the youngsters for 'double knacks', wide entries between each row of houses which lead into the next street.

Back on the Green going down from Bryant Street was a chemists by the name of Shenstone's, followed by the Co-Op, not only the grocers but also the Co-Op hair dressers. Janet King, later Johnson, travelled all the way from the Yew Tree at Yardley Wood, to learn her trade there. She was eventually to become manageress. After the Co-Op came Dyke's the bike shop (and Dinky toys I might add.) Dyke's were renowned all over the Green and down in Handsworth where they had another shop in Rookery Road opposite the Plaza Ballroom. Many an eager young face looked through his shop window to view the latest Claud Butler bike with 10 speed gears, also to spend a whole half crown on the latest Dinky model. Mr. Dyke didn't care how long you took deciding, as long as you were satisfied. The problem was that when you came out of the shop you wished you had chosen one of the others. Then came Mr. Gittin's who kept the fish and chip shop. Close by was Beck's the chemists, who also had another shop up by the corner of Heath Street. On the corner of Magdala Street was a haberdashers owned by Misses Cal and Overton. This must have been a haberdashery for a good many years as my grannie Bamford took my aunts, Mary and Alice, there to get their first overalls when they started work at Settern and Derwards. That must have been in 1936. I don't know whether those two ladies were there in 1936, but it shows how shops in those days didn't change their wares.

On the other side of the road was Mr. Docker and Dr. Johnson. Like all local doctors we felt that they had been around for ever. Over the practice was a dentist. I never went to him, like lots of kids at that time we were taken to the Dental Hospital in Great Charles Street. (I think that place put me off a dentist's chair for life).

Back up the Green and coming down from Aberdeen Street was Bryant's the furnishers. A few doors down was Payne's the shoe repairers, this shop was where Jim Wilson started work. In the 1950's 'Teddy Boys' were making their name felt, and the clothes to go with it. Zissman's in the town and Grooms down Smethwick were the two shops that I went to, but a lot of the lads off the Green went to Bob Smarts. Twelve inch bottoms and shocking pink socks. It makes today's styles seem drab in comparison. Pat Cutt's the electrical shop, where the latest radios and gramaphones could be bought. Below Pat Cutt's was Bob Spicer's the green grocers, then came Tay's the butchers and before the Smith's Arms was Edgington's who kept yet another general shop. Mr. Edgington also worked at the Museum in the town as an attendant. Last but not least came the Smith's Arms on the corner of Peel Street. The pub is still there. Everything else though around it has gone. The pub now has been re-named the Old Smithy. Perhaps people new to the area think that it had its own farrier at the rear at one time. Perhaps a distant descendant of Stringer's the penny wink man might have had his horses shod there. We'll never know. I certainly don't think by changing the name it changes the place.

I apologise if I've missed any shops out on our way down the Green, but those mentioned were the most talked about to me. Going further on down just before the canal bridge was Frank Cleveland the builders. This I shall leave for another time as I think this warrants a lot more.

We are now back on my territory, with a difference though. I've written about the shops and the area, I've mentioned the Winson Green picture house. I missed out one pub the last time round and that was the Acorn. Surprisingly that is the last pub on that road till you come onto the Soho Road ('Main Road' to the regulars) which is the Red Lion. This now brings me onto the one place which outsiders always seem to remind us of. The prison.

Looking down the 'Green' from the canal bridge.
The prison officers club is on the right and the blank space to the left where
once the Winson Green Picture Palace stood.
(by kind permission of Alan Dolman)

WINSON GREEN PALACE

WINSON GREEN ROAD, BIRMINGHAM.

PRICE ONE PENNY.
The proceeds from the sale of programmes
will be given to charity.

Manager and Licensee ——————————— A. W. Hall.
Proprietors ————— The Winson Green Picture Palace Ltd.

Directors :
F. H. Shakeshaft and F. H. Shakeshaft, Junr.
Telephone : Northern 1790.

47

Chapter 13
From sailors to firemen

To all intents and purposes Dave Avery was no different to any of us kids growing up after the war. I suppose that having a mom and dad that owned a shop in a hard working area of Birmingham seemed a bit of one upmanship to others. It wasn't so. Grief follows happiness. This is one story about countless little people who stayed 'little' and stayed happy, and at the same time took great pleasure in telling me the story of his family.

A young Dave Avery as an auxiliary fireman in the 60's.
(D. Avery)

A grandad who was a seaman and a fireman, and a gran on the other side of the family who came from a little lane in Burntwood, Staffordshire. A lane that didn't even have a name to it.

His father, he thinks, was born on a naval station, possibly Portsmouth in 1908. After grandad had left the navy he went as a full time fireman back in Birmingham. They lived in Kings Heath, at 55 Highbury Road. Dave seems to think that this was the home of the Barr family, who were well know pork butchers from that area. On the outbreak of war in 1914 his grandad was re-called into the navy and in 1917 was re-called once again to the fire service in Birmingham owing to a shortage of firemen. The name of Avery is well known to us from that side of Birmingham. After all the Soho Foundry in Smethwick was taken over by that family in 1896. (Dave in later years found out that his family were distant relations of to the Avery family. Not possibly on speaking terms but in genealogy.) Not till years later did another Avery family settle down the Green.

The Winson Green connection came from his gran on his mothers side. As I have said she was born down a lane in Burntwood. This was a literal fact.

48

The address on her birth certificate was "Close by the Nag's Head, Burntwood Staffordshire". As I have previously written on many occasions people from all walks of life came into Birmingham for a better life and this family were no different.

She and her husband by the name of Freeman, who had been a miner in the Cannock area, moved into Carlisle Street where Dave's mother was born and was christened Edna. She had a sister who I mentioned played the organ at the chapel in Peel Street. Somewhere along the line Len Avery came on the scene in the 1930's. After coming out of the army in the early 30's, he had a succession of local jobs. They were married in 1936 and had two sons John and

Len Avery as attendant to the Curator of the
Archaeology Department at Birmingham Museum.
(by kind permission of Dave Avery)

David.

In 1937 Dave Avery's parents opened a shop at 133 Peel Street. It was originally a small sweet shop, but they changed it to a haberdashery, and soon after incorporated a tobacconist as well. This though was not sufficient and Len Avery got a job at Birmingham Museum and Art Gallery as an attendant. War came and he was called up into the Air Force. After the war he returned to the museum. In 1950 he was promoted to technical assistant in the Archaeology

49

and Local History Department. He was made assistant to the keeper of the department Mr. Adrian Oswold. He continued there till his early demise in 1961 at the age of 53. His wife had at that time already passed on. This was to be a local talking point in the street for a long time to come. In 1958 his wife had died in very, very tragic circumstances.

The shop closed after her death. John, Dave and their dad continued living there till Dave left in 1960. Soon after Len died and John stayed there for a time then he moved out.

This little shop was never again to sell a piece of linen or a reel of cotton, or even a packet of fags. Never again to be a stopping off place for the local bobby to take a crafty drag in the confines of the shop.

Dave, who was born in 1940, went to school at Barford Road and Dudley Road and then came back to Barford Road. After leaving school in 1955 he went to work at Barlow's of Birmingham as a trainee typewriter mechanic. In 1960 he was married to Sheila Clemmens. She came out of Talbot Street Off Lodge Road. He joined the fire service as an auxiliary, while holding down a job at the same time with Dennison's the watch case company. Over the years he served in Birmingham and Staffordshire fire brigade as an auxiliary, and finished up in the ambulance service in Birmingham working alongside that well known author from Hockley, Ron 'Smudge' Smith.

Like a good many of us who left Birmingham in the 60's, Dave and his wife Sheila went to live out in the Brownhills area. Not really that spectacular but with a twist to the tale. They would be living within less than a mile to where, over a hundred years or more before, a baby was born down a lane with no number to the house! What comes round goes round, as the saying goes!

Chapter 14
A castle down Winson Green Road

None of us from Winson Green ever forgot the prison. We didn't notice it, for as with Walton in Liverpool, Strangeways in Manchester, Pentonville in London and other notables around the country, it was part of the area. It seemed like that it had always been there. It had the look of a castle that had been turned into a prison with it's high walls, it's castle turrets and round towers it could have come from Camelot, but it didn't. It was home for many a transgressor. It was part of a scheme. A prison, workhouse and an asylum (later on a hospital) all in one area. Why was it there? Well as they say, it had got to be somewhere. What more suitable place than an unproductive heathland doing nothing.

Let's start by finding out how we came to this conclusion and what started it all off. Let's start with the prison. The first of the known Birmingham prisons, was at the Leather Hall at the bottom of which is now New Street. Demolition of the Leather Hall in 1778 brought new demise of the towns dungeons, the towns first lock-up. It was replaced with another brideswell or prison in Peck Lane. Where now stands New Street Station. Hutton, the Birmingham historian, wrote at that time of Peck Lane, "Of all places, the worst". Even John Howard the prison reformer at that time was scathing about the conditions which were prevalent at the place in 1779. He recites in his findings of "two night rooms for women eight feet by five feet nine inches and other rooms over them. On the other side is the gaolers stable and one small day-room for men and women; no window". He also described the insanitary conditions and over crowding. When he re-visited the prison in 1788 not much had changed. "Only the court is paved with broad stones but dirty with fowls". Over the door to the one and only day room for both sexes was a sign 'Universal Academy' (political correctness was even noted then). At that time there was another prison in the Birmingham area at Aston. Possibly one of the worst in the country. It consisted of two subterranean dungeons reached through a trap door. Prisoners received an allowance of four pence a day and a rug to cover them.

Back in Peck Lane things were just a little less primitive. For 2/6d you got a bed in the gaoler's house, though unfortunately you were handcuffed to the bedstead. That is why we need to look at the gaoler's lot at that time. They weren't paid a salary, these prisons were usually adjoining a pub and the

51

gaoler's other job was as the publican, and he'd sell his wares to the locals and also the inmates! I spoke about the prison as Aston, even at that particular pub the dungeons were directly underneath. As was the Birmingham Brideswell in Peck Lane which served as an off-licence. It fulfiled a curious dual roll. This had all got to stop. Birmingham was growing and it needed some stabilisation. William Hutton suggested in 1780 that Peck Lane be closed down and demolished. His idea was to build a new gaol on the corner of Colmore Row and New Street! The street commissioners would have none of this and plans were laid down for a new gaol in Moor Street.

It opened in 1806. It was self contained and had the added advantage of a 26 foot wall, and most significant it had no off-licence adjoining. It remained the town's gaol for 40 years. An illustration shows what a grand ornate building it was. It combined the Public Office with the gaol, but was condemned for this. It didn't matter though for the first time in our city we had one building which encompassed an institution of the law, the poor law, and above all local government. Up until this time any felons who had transgressed on a larger scale had been sent to the county gaol at Warwick. This was not just costly but inconvenient. Birmingham, after 1839, had it's own quarter sessions. It's first convicted criminal was a Thomas Allen, he received two months hard labour for stealing a wooden bowl on the fifth of July, and he was sent to Warwick. This couldn't go on. So designs for a new prison were laid down. It was paramount. The ground was available on the Heath at Winson Green. Then it was all about building it. Plans were drawn up, and to be modelled on the Pentonville design. It would have 336 cells. There were to be many takers after the 17th of October 1849. It later increased to 612 cells in 1885. The total cost was upwards of £60,000. It was to be called the Borough Gaol.

The first governor was a Captain Maconochie RN. He was a reformer and adopted this attitude towards the prisoners. He didn't punish just for the sake of it. The second governor was also ex RN but with more of a vicious streak. He tried to create a training ship in our land locked city. He was Lieutenant Austin RN. Later on he was to be in a royal commission of enquiry over the matter of a prisoner committing suicide.

The young lad in question was Edward Andrews. He was only 15 years old. There had been numerous other suicide attempts before by previous inmates but this one was not to be covered up. The discipline meted out by Austin to any prisoner who broke the slightest rule, however, unintentionally was to be put on hard labour. For a prisoner to receive his three meals a day whilst on hard labour he would have to turn a meaningless crank 10,000 times a day. Young Andrews in the short time of two weeks had turned the crank 120,000 times! But still he hadn't completed his required amount and was put on bread and water, which weakened him further. He probably felt he had no other course of action than to take his own life in a very sad way.

The original Public Office in Moor Street possibly the late 1850's.
The site of Birmingham's first purpose built prison.
(Author's collection)

What more can we say. Winson Green's fame to notoriety. The Prison.
(A. Dolman)

Prisoners were questioned at the enquiry, the screw was beginning to turn. Austin as it came out was using straight jackets and leather collars, was strapping prisoners to the wall, dousing them with cold water, stuffing salt into mouths. All meted out for the slightest indiscipline. Governor Austin decided to resign prior to the enquiry findings, but to no avail. It didn't save him from prosecution. For all of this despicable treatment of prisoners, he received a pitiful three months imprisonment. I don't know if it was at the Green that he did his time. I would have been very surprised if it was.

The Green, like most major prisons, was a hanging prison. A public notice would be put in the notice board outside the main gates of the prison giving details of the impending execution, and on the day a bell would be rung at the given time. Times and days for executions varied.

I tried to find out who was the first to be hung at the new prison, but was unsuccessful. A friend of mine, John Cotten, who was a Senior Prison Officer at the jail, tried his utmost to find out, but to no avail as records didn't give the answer to the one question that I needed. Perhaps one day I shall be lucky. What we do know though is that the last execution was of Oswald Grey on the 20th of November 1962. There were to be only five other hangings in the country after this one. Up until 1942 8.00a.m. was the usual time for a hanging, after that it was changed to 9.00a.m. It changed again to 9.30a.m. in 1957.

In this century alone 33 men and one woman were hung at the 'Green'.

People much older than myself may remember a murder on the Green. The lady in question was Olive Turner who lived in Ford Street, Hockley. She and her boyfriend Charles Broomhead had been to the Winson Green picture house. They decided to walk home along the canal, which was a stone's throw away from the cinema. They turned off the Winson Green Road and along the tow path. Walking along towards Clissold Street they were stopped by a Thomas Power. He made believe that he was a policeman, and was going to arrest them for being on private property. All of their pleadings were to be of no avail. He then escorted them back along the canal towards the Winson Green Road where he told them that they were going to the police station. Broomhead had smelt a rat, as Power had intimated that he could be 'squared'. Broomhead had only fourpence on him and Power took out three half crowns from his pocket, and replied to the effect that a small amount of money as that was of no use to him. Broomhead told Olive to run home back along the canal towards Hockley. Upon this she took to her heels. Power chased after Olive and Broomhead ran after the two of them, fearful of what might happen to Olive. As he attempted to pass Power, Power turned around and swung a blow to Broomhead which knocked him out. When he came round neither of them were to be seen. He ran to Olive's house and told the story to the boy-friend of Olive's sister. They both ran back to the canal, and on the tow path of the branch towards the Soho Pool found remains of some of her belongings. They contacted the police and the next day the body of Olive Turner was found. Through eye witnesses a picture was made up and Thomas Power was subsequently identified and arrested as he left work at Canning's in Kenyon Street. After a short case, Thomas Power was convicted of killing Olive Turner and was given the death sentence in December of the same year. At 9.00a.m. on Tuesday the 31st of January 1928, Power was hung. The hangman being Thomas Pierrepoint. A crowd upwards of 2,000 gathered around the gates to the prison, from either sympathy or morbid curiosity. Power was the 14th person to be hung at the Green this century, but he certainly wasn't the last. As I've written, the final hanging was to be Oswald Grey in 1962 for the murder of Thomas Bates of Lea Bank.

The final bit of notoriety to add to this chapter was the escape of Charlie Wilson in 1965. He was one of the great train robbers of 1963. He was being held at Winson Green till his trial. He escaped over the wall onto the tow path at the back of the prison. He was later caught, but at the time there would have been a lot of red faces and searching questions to be had at the prison!

Looking further down the 'Green' towards Dolman's garage in the early 60's. On the right the former prison officer's houses are awaiting demolition.
(A. Dolman)

The prison governor's house on the corner of Winson Green Road and Lodge Road.
(A. Dolman)

Chapter 15
A house older than the prison

Anyone from Winson Green knows where Dolmans garage is. My old mate Bob is the fourth son of this lovely family, and the present owner of the garage is Alan. A third generation is now helping to keep the name going, Stuart and Adrian. This all sounds rather unremarkable, not unlike any other up and coming business in our city that started after the war, but this is not so. The story that I will now tell is not just about a business, but about a little bit of important property and the way this family built up possibly the most well known name in the area.

Before the war the house was owned by a Doctor O'Dowd. Not until 1945 was the house occupied by Mr. and Mrs. Dolman. It was in a run down state and lots of energy and money would have to go into it before it could be a viable proposition. So let us learn something about this one particular family.

Mr. Dolman Snr. came out of Bacchus Road. Those who can remember that particular spot will recall a small triangular plot of houses, a path went behind these, down some steps into Lodge Road. He was crippled as a baby when a young girl accidentally dropped him on his back-side. Medical knowledge wasn't as advanced as it is today and he was left with a shortened right leg owing to the hip joint coming out of its socket.

As he was always keen on cars, when he grew older he eventually owned one. But he would have to have the car modified for a hand throttle. When his sons grew up and wanted to learn how to drive, they would have to learn foot and hand throttles. The way he rigged his cars out was unique. Everything from a Morris 8 to an Aston Martin were all dual throttled! Even in 1955 the Aston Martin, which he owned, was used as a towing truck in emergencies. Everything that moved was used for the business. No posing in those days.

Mrs. Dolman's parents came from Bodmin in Cornwall, and settled in Beeton Road. They kept a hucksters shop, selling sweets and home-made ice-cream. Mr. and Mrs. Dolman got married and lived with her parents there. During the war she was a milk lady delivering milk for Handsworth Dairies as well as bringing up a family.

They took on the lease of the house and also the adjoining building in 1945 for the rent of £5 a week. The house, as I have said, was in a bad way. The glass in the windows was broken, the paintwork was peeling and the wallpaper was falling off the walls. Mind you they did have one advantage. If the tap didn't work in the scullery there was a well underneath for emergencies. To this day the well is still there. Mr. and Mrs. Dolman had moved from out of Beeton Road. The boys though continued to live with their nan and grandad for a short time till the house was made habitable. Afterwards they made their way up to the garage and their new home.

Their one main room was at the back next to the scullery. One room at a time was done up. While this was going on Mr. Dolman was still working at the S.U. Carburettor at Cosford. He was eventually made redundant. As he was a keen lover of the motor car, he decided to open up a garage. Even though he was completely under experienced and under capitalised he still went ahead. The incentive, I suppose, was the fact he had four growing lads. Not only was a he very keen mechanic but his trade was as a jeweller, and he was an accomplished musician in his own right. These other interests he had to pack up as the garage was beginning to take off. In 1946 the first of the holes were dug for the petrol tanks. This wasn't a case, as in these days, of fetching in contractors to do the dirty work. this was all self help. (no J.C.B.'s!) Mrs. Dolman would get the lads ready for school, pack them off and muck in. When the lads came home they would have to do the same, till the hole was finished. Then the 500 gallon tank was put in. This was accomplished with the help of a builder by the name of Frank Cole who at one time lived in Perrot Street. When they eventually got going the need was for a second pump, then a second tank was put in. Things started to take off and it was a case of all hands to the pumps. (excuse the pun, Ed.) John who was the eldest and attended Handsworth Grammar School was no exception, he would have to come home from school, have his tea and with all of his brothers serve the petrol. This was probably till 10 o'clock at night. (including Christmas day). An old air raid shelter was converted into a bay with an inspection ramp.

It was, I'm told, the first garage in Birmingham to get a licence to sell petrol after the war.

Mind you there was another car repair business close at hand, but this one closed down tragically. On the corner of Foundry Road and Franklin Street was a shop and at the back was another car repair business which was run by a father and son by the name of Bailey. The son was in a unique accident. He was only young , and whilst repairing a car sitting on his backside the car tipped off the jack, ran into the work bench and broke his neck. The father then gave the business up. Just afterwards it was turned into an engineering shop ran by a little company called Stovil Engineering.

Dolman's garage is just across the road from the prison. Their customers naturally came into the garage, from the prison governor down to the warders, even some of the inmates when released. Alan told me the story of the duty that some of the local business men would have to carry out on the day of the hanging. This was during the late 40's and 50's. At times Pierrepoint who was visiting the prison to do his gruesome job would leave his car at Dolman's. During his stay he would stop at the Acorn public house. Mr. Dolman was required, amongst others, to witness not the actual hanging but the deceased prisoner after he had been taken down. They were paid the grand sum of 2/6d. Not exactly a pleasant job to do but as I've said it was a duty. After the hanging he would come back over to the garage, give Mr. Dolman a 10/- note (50p) for looking after his car, which Alan remembers as a silver Sunbeam Talbot, fill up with petrol and off he would go. Possibly to another prison and another hanging. There were other hangmen who 'visited' the prison. People such as Samuel Plant, Harry Allen and Stephen Wade. Alan Dolman though remembers Albert Pierrepoint, who took his trade from his father Thomas, more than the rest. I suppose they also left their cars at the garage, and also had to do the gruesome job over at the prison, and for the likes of Mr. Dolman and other shop keepers such as Mr. Willey, Mr. Clutterbuck, Williams the greengrocer and Tommy Wheeler they would continue to do their civic duty on the appointed day. This would finish in 1962 at the Green and in the country as a whole three years later.

This is where we need to get back to the story. During the 50's after buying the premises, he had to sell the other part to pay a tax bill. This part was bought by the Elim Church. It was a shame though as it was made into one big house and today the connecting doors can still be seen through the plasterwork. The house is remarkable. Now let me give the reader a little bit of history concerning this lovely pile which was known as the Gables and still is.

The history of this particular house starts in the early part of the 19th century when a button manufacturer by the name of James Turner had a house built on what would now be Foundry Road Schools. His premises would have been in the town, and like all wealthy merchants moved out to what would then have been known as the country. It was to be a house of quite a stature. With manicured gardens and a large vista down what is now James Turner and Perrot Streets. The property was built in the first part of the 1800's. Nothing though remains of the big house. The schools in Foundry Road and the two streets were built on the area. Only perhaps for some old photographs in the library, there is nothing to remind us at all.

This wasn't the house in question. The house that the Dolman's lived in was the gate house. It was two houses together. Each with it's own front door. Possibly a game keeper and the head gardener. We aren't to know. What we do know is that this property was much older than the prison and perhaps one of the first properties to be built in Winson Green of any size. As far as I can find out the main house was called Winson House and the one that we are talking about was Winson Green House. We know this from the Post Office Directory of 1845 which gave that address to a James Boyle Esq. Somebody who was living there then makes this property older than the prison, which we know hadn't begun to be built until the end of 1845.

So there we have it. A little bit of history from down the bottom of the Green. The house still stands proud, facing Lodge Road. It has been there for the past 150 odd years, and by the look of it, it will probably go round again.

Mrs. Dolman making her way across the garage forecourt in the 50's. Beyond the pumps stands a remaining pillar to the entrance to Winson House the home of James Turner in the 1850's. (A. Dolman)

Mr. Dolman with one of his original vans in the late 40's. (A. Dolman)

Looking up the Green from the garage.

The houses older than the 'Green'.
(A. Dolman)

Chapter 16
Back to Foundry Road School

While talking to the many people who came from up the Green, it was surprising to find out that there were quite a few children who came out of streets off the Winson Green Road and who went to Foundry and Handsworth New Road Schools. The usual schools would have been Barford Road and Dudley Road. The Catholics though would have gone to St. Patrick's. Because of this I couldn't resist coming back to my first school.

Hilda Smith, who was to marry a fellow teacher by the name of Geoff Thomas, bought my first book and got in touch with me. She was the teacher who taught me all those years ago in junior school, well not just me but hundreds of children from around the area. The photo's that go with this chapter will bring back no end of memories to a lot of people from up and down the Green I am sure.

The school was built in 1883. It was to accommodate 1002 pupils. A charge was made for each pupil of twopence for children up to seven and threepence for those who were older up to the leaving age of 13. The younger ones were charged a penny soon after. In poorer districts the figure was a penny all round. The school was not formally opened till 1886. I found that out as the school held its centenary in 1986. As with others, it was a board school run by the City Education Department. It is situated between Perrot and James Turner Streets. In the area at that time there were only three other board schools. One of those was in Smethwick, at Slow Lane. (Re-named Wellington Street in the last years of the 19th century). The other one was the Dudley Road School. Handsworth New Road and Barford Road schools were to come along later. So here we can see where the children were taught, not by choice of schools but where they lived. This perhaps was the reason why children coming from the area below the railway lines on the Winson Green Road went to Foundry Road whilst those from above that point went to Dudley Road. This wasn't always to follow but in my findings this seemed to be the general pattern.

At that time children would have gone to the same school from five years of age till leaving at the allotted age of the time. This was to change over the years, as more schools were built and the leaving age was gradually raised. This was to be the same for Foundry Road and the remainder of schools of that type across the city. Naturally if a child was bright there were always the grammar schools. My own dad passed the necessary tests to be admitted, but unfortunately his mom couldn't afford the uniform. No social service help in those days.

The school was built to the usual design. With high vaulted ceilings and classrooms radiating from the main halls. The school is actually two side by side. Even though this was a mixed school, there were two entrances, one for the girls and the other for the boys. They were built austere, and were meant to look that way. This was formal education and a virtual fear was put into any new pupil. The fear of going into school for the first time, and also the fear of not going again.

When I was young there was always the official known as the school-board man. Whether or not this man was real he was known to me as Mr. Harris. Just the mention of his name put the fear of God into us. I know we never knocked a day off school.

After the war, we children of school age started there. I won't go on to talk about myself as I've already mentioned my memories in my first book. We've all got memories of our teachers, some we got to know better than others. Hilda Smith was one as I've remarked and a good one at that.

It must have been different after the war with a new government in. Things were changing. It was going to be a brighter start. A new National Health Service, an education act that would alter all manner of things over the coming years and a lot more changes to come. It was to be different from the lean 30's. It would now be the teaching staff across all spectrums to put words into actions.

To us kids though we weren't to know. It was a case of going to that school, and whether we wanted to or not we were going to be taught.

Hilda Smith (I'll use her maiden name for now) came to Foundry Road Juniors as her first teaching post after leaving college. Upon this she learned from Miss Moyle the rudiments of teaching in her own words. Hilda thought she was a wonderful head and ran an extremely good school. Hilda taught from September 1951 till April 1955 when she married a fellow teacher by the name of Geoff Thomas. Unfortunately they left Birmingham and moved to Leicester. She was born and bred in Handsworth. She attended Rookery Road and later George Dixon's in City Road. Her journeys to George Dixon's would take her through Winson Green by various routes on her bike. In 1947 during the heavy snows she still made her way up the Green, this time without her bike. It was a good excuse for being late. More often though it was the outer circle bus that she used.

We as children growing up would look at our teachers and perhaps for the want of a better word think that they were millionaires. Well the men always wore a suit and the ladies smart dresses. Our dads coming from work looked scruffy in comparison, and our moms only seemed to look lovely on high days and holidays. Behind this though they probably had a similar background.

Hilda's maternal grandmother lived in Handsworth. A very strong character, who had an extremely hard life having been widowed with three small children, even though she was only in her 20's, she lived in a back to back house on the Dudley Road and had to put the two boys, the youngest, into Princess Alice Orphanage. Her mother she managed to keep. Hilda seems to recall that her mom was looked after by family whilst her gran went to work. She worked at Nettlefold's. Social benefits were non existent at the turn of the century, it was either to grub a living as best as you could, or face the walk down Western Road to the municipal workhouse. Hilda still has the stool which was made for her gran when she was at Nettlefold's. No it wasn't for sitting on, it was because she was so small that she couldn't reach her machine! So much for heath and safety. She never really got to know her gran well, as she died when Hilda was only 10 years old.

All of us who went to Foundry Road remember Miss Moyle, a forward looking headmistress. It was not to be just the three R's, but to experience and enjoy a wider world. So children from Winson Green were to sing in music festivals in Birmingham Town Hall, took part in athletics at Mitchell's and Butler's sports ground at Cape Hill, and also fielded football, cricket and skittleball teams. Once a year there was the annual trip which the whole school took part in, the caretaker, Mr. Whiting and his wife, the school secretary and even the dinner ladies went. Hilda remembers trips to Billing Aquadrome and Alton Towers (it would take more than a few shillings to get into there today). The most ambitious trip to date was to New Brighton. Early one morning the whole school trooped up the Green to get the train from Winson Green Road railway station to Liverpool. At the other end, a long line of children and teachers made their way to the pier head. After a ride on the Liverpool Dock Railway they took the ferry across to New Brighton and the sands. Tea was held in a large hall, and if you went to the seaside it had got to be fish and chips. The way back was different again as they came back by bus through the Mersey Tunnel and to Lime Street station. Then the return journey back to the Green. To some of those children it was perhaps the first time they had seen the sea, but to them all it was was a great day out, and all credit to those involved.

I have said on numerous occasions that we can all remember some of our teachers, by memory and the years that would pass, names and faces would dim. I wrote that I owed a gratitude to a Mr. Cross. Until Hilda sent me some photographs of the teaching staff I couldn't really put a name to their faces. Like a lightbulb going on I found I knew them all. It was as if 40 odd years had never been. Over the years most of them left our city. Hilda after marrying Geoff Thomas loved to Leicester, Miss Pamela Powell lives in Weston-Super-Mare, Ray Lewis left the Green and moved to Street in Somerset where he became a head teacher. Of the others I'm waiting to find out. One though stopped locally and that was Vic Kirkham. He was deputy head or chief assistant (as they were then known). He then went on to be headmaster of Saint James' in Sandwell Road, Handsworth. Here are the rest of the staff from possibly 1954. Dave Jenkins, Dave Cummings, Mr. Eames, Eric Cross, Ray Lewis, Miss Wastell and Peggy Dunn. One that we shall never forget and that was Miss Moyle. After leaving school life, she and her sister moved to Christchurch in Dorset. Hilda had kept in touch till the 1980's. Not hearing from her again she thinks she has since died. Perhaps to us though she'll never pass on, or be forgotten.

The school is still there, it looks the same as it always did. Now it's another team of workers who will do their utmost to educate another generation of Winson Green children.

Foundry Road School in the early 1950's (note the tram lines).
(by kind permission of Geoff Thomas)

Class of the Coronation year 1953 at Foundry Road Junior School
(G. Thomas)

The staff at Foundry Road Juniors in 1952.
(G. Thomas)

Endpiece
From the top to the bottom

From Sammy Small to Dolman's garage, we've been there. The streets have changed now. Where once there were back-to-back houses and trams, there are now detached ones on the same spot with one or more cars on the drives. The trams had given way to buses in the 40's. Now I can't figure out the new route numbers, and the directions from where they are going to or coming from.

The Dudley Road doesn't feel the same now. Shops and businesses, which we all knew have changed but it is still a very busy shopping area. Still full of hustle and bustle. Pity though that the Grove and Hawley's have closed their doors. The shops have all gone from down the Winson Green Road, even the Congregational Church opposite the prison is up for sale.

The old prison facade has been changed, no first impression of a castle but of a modern American style penitentiary. It still doesn't alter the area. There is still, as I have said, the prison and of course the hospital, even though that has very recently changed it's name from Dudley Road to the City Hospital.

A lot of the pubs have gone now. Those still open stand out like a sore thumb. Like the Queen's Head in Aberdeen Street, all the houses have long gone, but the pub still stands on the pavement. The pubs in this story were all real, with real people, no background music (unless we count a piano) or a pool table. It was a place to go to for a bit of company. Domino and darts teams would visit other pubs in the area. When the houses were pulled down and the people moved all over Birmingham it seemed that this would be the final story, but naturally it isn't as one moves out another moves in.

The area though will never die. It has left us all with a lot of thoughts and memories. Long live the Green.

By the same author:

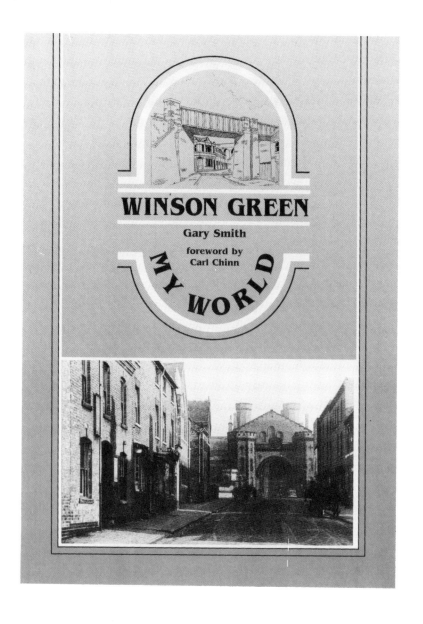

WINSON GREEN

Gary Smith

foreword by
Carl Chinn

MY WORLD